TIME NOW FOR THE
VINYL CAFE
STORY EXCHANGE

STUART McLEAN

TIME NOW FOR THE
VINYL CAFE
STORY EXCHANGE

VIKING

VIKING
an imprint of Penguin Canada Books Inc.

Published by the Penguin Group
Penguin Canada Books Inc.
90 Eglinton Avenue East, Suite 700, Toronto, Ontario, Canada M4P 2Y3

Penguin Group (USA) Inc., 375 Hudson Street, New York, New York 10014, U.S.A.
Penguin Books Ltd, 80 Strand, London WC2R 0RL, England
Penguin Ireland, 25 St Stephen's Green, Dublin 2, Ireland (a division of Penguin Books Ltd)
Penguin Group (Australia), 707 Collins Street, Melbourne, Victoria 3008, Australia
(a division of Pearson Australia Group Pty Ltd)
Penguin Books India Pvt Ltd, 11 Community Centre, Panchsheel Park,
New Delhi – 110 017, India
Penguin Group (NZ), 67 Apollo Drive, Rosedale, Auckland 0632, New Zealand
(a division of Pearson New Zealand Ltd)
Penguin Books (South Africa) (Pty) Ltd, 24 Sturdee Avenue, Rosebank,
Johannesburg 2196, South Africa

Penguin Books Ltd, Registered Offices: 80 Strand, London WC2R 0RL, England

First published 2013

1 2 3 4 5 6 7 8 9 10 (RRD)

Copyright © Stuart McLean, 2013

The Vinyl Cafe is a registered trademark.

Manufactured in the U.S.A.

Library and Archives Canada Cataloguing in Publication data available
upon request to the publisher.

ISBN: 978-0-670-06475-5

Visit the Penguin Canada website at **www.penguin.ca**

Special and corporate bulk purchase rates available; please see
www.penguin.ca/corporatesales or call 1-800-810-3104, ext. 2477.

It is my belief that if enough of us write, and if we tell the truth about some small thing, we will create a snapshot of our country—an archive of sorts—a picture of who we are, how we feel about things, and most importantly, what we feel is important.

—Stuart McLean, September 2003

CONTENTS

YEAR TWO

YEAR THREE

YEAR FOUR

YEAR FIVE

YEAR SIX

YEAR SEVEN

YEAR EIGHT

YEAR NINE

YEAR TEN

INTRODUCTION

Ten years ago I asked listeners of The Vinyl Cafe *to send me their stories. "They have to be true," I said. "And they have to be short … but after that they don't have to be anything at all; after that it's up to you." The stories came in by the thousands.* The Vinyl Cafe Story Exchange *became a regular segment on the show. It is one of my favourite parts of the program. On the tenth anniversary of the Story Exchange I sat down with Jess Milton, producer of* The Vinyl Cafe, *to reminisce.*

Stuart: Do you remember when it started?

Jess: I remember exactly when it started.

Stuart: It was on my boat, right?

Jess: No, it wasn't on your boat.

Stuart: It was.

Jess: No.

Stuart: It was totally on my boat. I remember the day exactly.

Jess: No. You … you always get this confused. In your mind, the planning session … I guess we should back up and say we have a planning session every year.

Stuart: Yeah.

Jess: And in your mind we had one magical planning session on your boat where every good idea we've ever had came from.

Stuart: That's right.

Jess: But that planning session, the one where you think we came up with the idea for the Story Exchange, was my first year producing the show, and the Story Exchange started *before* I was producing it. The Story Exchange started my first year as production assistant.

Stuart: So where do *you* think it happened? Where do *you* think we came up with the idea?

Jess: I know exactly what happened, how it started.

Stuart: Okay. Tell me.

Jess: You were down in the States. On book tour. And when you came back you had a book.

Stuart: The *National Story Project*.

Jess: That's right. You handed me the book and you said, "There's something here that we could do on our show." And I said, "Okay, well, like what?" And you said, "That's your job," or something to that effect.

Stuart: Yeah.

Jess: And so I took it home and read the stories. And we talked about it. I don't remember that whole middle part.

Stuart: That was the part that happened on the boat.

Jess: No, no, it wasn't. You didn't even own a boat yet. You didn't own a boat for two more years. This is so easy to prove. We can go back and look at when you purchased the boat, and I can guarantee that the Story

Exchange started before you owned your little boat. So it's time for you to get over the whole boat thing.

Stuart: Yeah, you're right.

Jess: So then we got together one night. I think Dave Amer was there too. In your office at the old house on Madison.

Stuart: You were sitting on the floor.

Jess: That's exactly right. And you had that weird chair with the sticky arms and you used to pick at the arms like you were a rodent …

Stuart: More like a teething puppy …

Jess: And—

Stuart: I actually didn't pick at it. It just, sort of, disappeared. It was—

Jess: Magical?

Stuart: It was kind of falling apart.

Jess: Anyway, we tossed around ideas and we didn't quite get it. We talked for a long time, the three of us, and we came up with a bunch of ideas. You had a bulletin board by your desk. You pinned them on the board.

Stuart: The ideas?

Jess: Yeah. And you had come up with … you got really close. Like, you knew it should have the word "story" in it.

Stuart: Oh, we were talking about titles?

Jess: Yes.

Stuart: But what about the idea of people writing in stuff?

Jess: Oh, that was your idea.

Stuart: Okay.

Jess: Yeah. I mean, it was pretty obvious from the …

Stuart: From the go.

Jess: Yeah.

Stuart: We'd have people write in their stories.

Jess: Yeah, yeah.

Stuart: And then we were struggling to get a name?

Jess: We thought we'd start with a name and that would help us define what we were doing.

Stuart: Sort of backwards.

Jess: I don't think it's that backwards. We started with "They have to be short and they have to be true."

Stuart: Was that us?

Jess: You stole that from Paul Auster.

Stuart: No, I don't think I stole it.

Jess: Mm-hm.

Stuart: No, I don't think—

Jess: Yeah—

Stuart: I think I have the book right over on that shelf, we could probably check. I don't think he said it had to be short and true.

Jess: Yeah. Yeah, he did.

Stuart: I don't think so. I think you'll find it's different.

Jess: I think you'll find I'm right.

Stuart: Okay.

Jess: So we had that, we knew … they had to be true.

Stuart: Yeah.

Jess: And they had to be short, we knew that.

Stuart: Yeah.

Jess: And we didn't really know what else they had to be. You had the idea of The Moment. When you were a teacher, you described The Moment thing.

Stuart: Oh, yeah, yeah. My favourite writing exercise. I used to send my students out of the classroom. I wanted them to describe, in about a page, a perfect distilled moment. And the directions I came up with were "Tell me a story, about *someone,* doing *something, somewhere.*" They had to have all three elements: a character, a place, and an action. If they got all three they were almost guaranteed to write something beautiful. A little observation piece. Like you used to see in *The New Yorker* in the old days.

Jess: I disagree with that because, to me, the most interesting stories aren't about something, they're about the moment just before the something happens. Think about when you're having an emotional conversation with someone. The moment, say, just before they start crying is always more powerful than the tears themselves. That moment, the moment when things could go either way, is more interesting than the moment when things actually happen.

Stuart: Well. In that case the thing that happened is the conversation.

Jess: Okay. Good point.

Stuart: And that's what we wanted people to do. To describe a moment they had experienced, or witnessed, or heard about. We said it could be a moment of kindness or cruelty, of sadness or frivolity, a moment they were proud of or a moment they were ashamed of. It might not even be about them. It might be about someone they knew or maybe about someone they didn't know at all. Something that made them smile, or cry. Happy or sad. A photo of life, but taken with words instead of film.

Jess: So we had that much but, as always with you, you wanted a title. You love titles. You love defining things by titles.

Stuart: Yeah.

Jess: So you were stuck on the title.

Stuart: Finding a name for it.

Jess: Yeah.

Stuart: I was totally right. When we got the title—

Jess: That's exactly right. I remember thinking, Why are we focusing on the title? But you were right. Once we got the title, we had the concept. You had the word "story."

Stuart: And I said we needed a word that goes with the word "story."

Jess: Yeah, yeah.

Stuart: You came up with it, didn't you? "Exchange."

Jess: Eventually. I remember how that happened. I came home and was thinking about the idea of sharing. And I knew the word "sharing" was too lame. Too soft.

Stuart: Mm-hm, too sucky.

Jess: Yeah, but that's really what we're doing. Sharing stories. So I was playing around with the word "share." And I was thinking about other things you share with people. And I thought about my own life. And I remember thinking, What do I share with people? And the first thing I came up with was recipes, because that's something I do a lot: share recipes.

Stuart: Right.

Jess: And that got me to "recipe exchanging," which is a phrase you use.

Stuart: Mm-hm.

Jess: "Exchange" has weight and substance.

Stuart: Yeah, it hasn't been cheapened. The word "sharing" has been emotionally cheapened.

Jess: But it came from that, because that's really what it is.

Stuart: I remember you telling me the word. And me saying right away—

Jess: "Perfect."

Stuart: That's it, perfect.

Jess: Yeah. So—

Stuart: Once we had the title—

Jess: It was … discussion was over.

Stuart: This is going to work.

Jess: Our first show with the Story Exchange had five … I think five stories.

Stuart: Oh, that's right. I don't know how we did that.

Jess: And right away we got it. That it should only be *one* story per show.

Stuart: Mm. I'm proud of it.

Jess: Yeah. I think it's a nice idea because people love hearing your stories, but now *you're* hearing *their* stories.

Stuart: Yeah.

Jess: And I love that. When someone gives you a great gift, you desperately want to find the perfect gift to give them to show them how much *their* gift meant to you. And that's, sort of, what I feel happened with the Story Exchange. When we put the call out, we got a lot of letters. I don't know for sure how many but—

Stuart: Thousands.

Jess: Oh, my gosh. We've received thousands for sure, thousands within the first year alone.

Stuart: Yeah.

Jess: And what that said to me—and it's probably easier for me to say this than you—what that said to me is that people really love what you do. They love your stories and they have stories of their own that they want to share with you. You always talk about the moment of giving and receiving, and how you're so lucky, as an author, because you get to be there when your audience receives what you've written. Well, with the Story Exchange, it's the same for them. How cool is that?

Stuart: Mm, mm.

Jess: I think that's great. So I like that about the Story Exchange but I also like this idea of people getting a sense of how other people live.

Stuart: A lot of people tell us it's their favourite part of the show—

Jess: I love when they applaud—

Stuart: When?

Jess: In the live shows. When you say, "Time now for *The Vinyl Cafe* Story Exchange."

Stuart: Me too.

Jess: What's your favourite one?

Stuart: Well, I know yours. Yours is … I don't remember the guy's name, but it's the teacher.

Jess: Mr. Fisher.

Stuart: Mr. Fisher. Yeah. Mr. Fisher, the teacher. Well, I like "Fat Cat."

Jess: "Fatso …"

Stuart: "Fatso, the Cat."

Jess: One of the best.

Stuart: It was a great, funny one. And it has that great line in it.

Jess: If you wrote that line yourself you'd be thrilled.

Stuart: I'd be proud of it, yeah. I like the one about peeing off the side of the truck.

Jess: Oh, that was one of the early ones—the hitchhiking story.

Stuart: Is that A.J.?

Jess: No, that was Matthew Jackson. Matthew Jackson of …

Stuart: Somewhere out West.

Jess: He ended up writing a book, that guy.

Stuart: We've made some friends … A.J. Mittendorf.

Jess: A.J. Mittendorf has had two stories on the Story Exchange. There's only been a few people who've had more than one story. A.J. had the one about the birthday suit and the girl and the cookies—

Stuart: He's the master of the one-liner.

Jess: "Here. Catch."

Stuart: Yeah.

Jess: And he also had one we call "Freudian Slip."

Stuart: Oh, yeah, with the wind.

Jess: He used to live in Prince George, B.C. And, yeah, he's become a friend. He plays the bass. So he comes to the shows and he and Dennis Pendrith, our bass player, have jammed together a couple of times.

Stuart: You're kidding.

Jess: No, they—

Stuart: They jam together?

Jess: Yeah. A.J. has come up onstage and Dennis has shown him a few things and …

Stuart: What, after the show?

Jess: Yeah, yeah, after the show.

Stuart: Some of the stories have really moved me. Some of them have brought me to tears.

Jess: Some of them are very powerful. Some of them are funny. Some of them are just exactly what you asked for: a moment. And together I think they add up nicely to … I don't know … something bigger. What I learned, from reading not only these stories but the thousands that have come in over the past decade, is that the small stuff matters. The everyday experiences that we have with other people leave a lasting impact. And I like that because it means that we, and our actions, matter to others. We make a difference, even when we don't realize we're doing it.

Stuart: What do you want the collection to add up to?

Jess: I think of each story as a Polaroid picture, a little snapshot. And I want it to add up to some sort of family album. It doesn't need to tell some sort of story. It just has to leave the reader with a sense of what life was life was like for people, for our audience, during this decade. I want them to feel like they've been talking to a friend, that they've just had coffee with one of their friends ... You know that feeling you have after that, where you feel ...

Stuart: Connected.

Jess: Yeah. That you have a story to tell and someone to hear it.

Stuart: And life is good.

AIR MAIL

YEAR
ONE

THE MONGOOSE

Last year I bought a caged mongoose at a yard sale.

To be honest, it wasn't a real mongoose and the cage was actually a wooden box. It had a spring-loaded mechanism that propelled a fur stole out of the top. The whole thing was like a child's jack-in-the box, except for a small wire-mesh covering on the top. It gave you a fleeting glimpse at what *appeared* to be a vicious cobra killer.

It was the ultimate practical joke machine.

I did my best to sucker in anyone I could find. And all my victims responded in pretty much the same way:

"Oh my god, I think I'm going to have a heart attack."

Immediately followed by, "That's sick."

And within thirty seconds: "Hey, has my wife/friend/ mother-in-law seen this yet?"

Friends and neighbours called to borrow my mongoose machine or asked me to bring it to their homes.

One Sunday afternoon, when my neighbour was hosting a brunch for some of the members of his church, I got a phone call to bring over the mongoose and show some of his friends my exotic "pet."

One by one, every curious guest trundled down to the basement to have their wits scared out of them and then eagerly ascended the stairs to set up the next mark. At some point the congregation's minister arrived and was directed downstairs by one of his parishioners. As he approached the mongoose he told me matter-of-factly that he had ministered in Southeast Asia in his youth and was well aware of the mongoose's vicious reputation.

I had a live one here.

The minister had taken the bait and it was time to set the hook. I explained that, as he probably already knew *from his travels,* a mongoose is nocturnal so there was little to fear opening the cage during the day. Then I added, "But you wouldn't catch me opening this at night."

I sprang the latch on the cage and the bedraggled swatch of fur catapulted out the top.

The minister was no young man, but in two or three steps he put at least ten metres between us. When he looked back at his attacker he quickly realized it was a practical joke. His stare burned into my soul and he began his rebuke: "Young man, I find it virtually incomprehensible that you would take delight in preying upon the primordial fears of your fellow man, only to satisfy your own shallow desires."

I felt a stab of guilt.

As I struggled to mount my defence, two of his parishioners appeared at the top of the stairwell. The good reverend turned to them and in a kindly voice said, "Hello Mary, hello Dave. Have you two ever seen a real mongoose? Here, let me show you something interesting."

Rod Fuller

Waterloo, Ontario

SUNLIGHT ON LEAVES

Nancy and I became best friends two weeks after I moved into the big house on Duncan Street. She appeared at our door one morning wearing one of her smocked dresses and with her braids tied with crisp ribbons. She introduced herself to my mother.

"I'm Nancy Jane MacBeth," she said. "I heard you have a little girl my age and I would like to be her friend."

It was 1941. We were both five years old.

Nancy and I became fast friends. We both had vivid imaginations, so every day was an adventure. We played house, school, and office. We loved to colour and bake mud pies in the sunshine.

One day we came up with a wonderful idea—every Monday for the rest of our lives we would give each other a gift.

My first gift to her was a ring with a blue stone. It cost five cents—half of my weekly allowance. Oh, the excitement that first Monday when we exchanged small boxes! What gift would I get from Nancy? A ring? A brooch? A hair ribbon? But all I found in the box was a flower—a dark purple pansy resting on a bed of cotton batting.

"It's just a pansy," I said, disappointment in my voice.

"But it's special," Nancy answered. "Feel it … it's as soft as velvet."

I can remember only two other gifts I bought for Nancy with my pennies—a hair clip with bluebirds on it and a "genuine" cricket clicker. I can't recall any of the others. But I can remember what she gave me: half a newly hatched robin's egg, a special hiding place in Mrs. MacKenzie's hedges for those summer games of hide-and-seek, a nest of naked, pink baby mice in an old crate in the storage shed (we sat as quiet as mice ourselves and watched them), and a spider's web, under construction.

One very special gift was permission to sit on her own private branch of the huge birch tree in her backyard. I looked up to see the sunshine falling in bits and pieces through the leaves and looked down to see the patterns of sun and shade on the grass. I heard the ocean for the first time in a cowry shell in her father's study and saw the sunset through the rose-coloured glass of the round window on the front stair landing.

Eventually I tired of the gift giving. I complained to my mother, "Every week I buy Nancy a nice present from the store and she just gives me things I can't keep."

"Are you sure?" my mother asked. "It sounds to me as if she's given you some very special gifts."

"But they're not real presents," I insisted.

Nancy and I had a falling out over the whole thing. It was a nasty, name-calling fight that five-year-olds excel at. We cancelled the "best friends for life" clause and I went home and ground the robin's eggshell into a fine blue powder.

A year later Nancy was killed in a traffic accident. She was seven years old.

But Nancy's gifts remain. Every spring as I stoop to feel the velvet faces of the pansies in my garden I think of her. I carefully pick up the pieces of a robin's egg should I find them. And while I no longer climb trees, I never pass under a birch tree without looking up to see the sunlight playing on the leaves.

At five, Nancy knew the secret of giving gifts that truly last a lifetime. How blessed I am to have had her for a friend.

Enid Vallis

Naramata, British Columbia

HEIGHT OF HUMANITY

I don't know what my father did in the war. Except that he entered as a private, and left as a master sergeant.

He was a pattern-cutter in the garment industry in New York when he volunteered for service. By volunteering, he was able to choose the Signal Corps. It was thought that this would offer an extra measure of safety, but it did not. Someone in command had a brainwave. When the first marine hit the beach on each of the island-hopping Pacific invasions, a working telephone should be waiting. Installing that telephone line was my father's job.

By the time I was old enough to understand my father's war stories, he'd stopped talking about the war. My brother, who's five years older than I am, heard all his terrifying tales of blood-curdling banzai charges in the jungle night, and of men leaping into foxholes to escape the machine-gun bullets of strafing Mitsubishi Zeros.

But there was one war story my father did continue to tell. About how, one night, he did *not* shoot a looter. He was guarding a supply dump on one of the Philippine islands. A young Filipino boy was running away with a case of something held over his head. My father said he shouted the warning, "Stop, or I'll shoot!" The Filipino boy, never breaking stride, replied, "I am not the one." My father laughed. He laughed whenever he retold that tale, and it was the only war story he ever told in his later years.

That story never seemed especially heroic to me when I was a boy. But now that I'm no longer young, it seems to me to be the very height of humanity and good sense.

My father died in 1995. There are, almost certainly, no military medals awarded for *not* shooting a looter, for *not* killing a starving, terrified boy in his own war-ravaged country, but maybe there should be.

Bob Friedland

Richmond, British Columbia

A LONG WAY
TO LONGLAC

When Jimmy Robbins was twenty he attended Lakehead University in Thunder Bay. Jimmy was from Newfoundland. He used to thumb his way back home at Christmastime.

Northern Ontario was the most difficult leg of Jimmy's trip. There are only two roads that cross that part of the province, the Trans-Canada and Highway 11. Both of them are surly. Experience quickly taught Jimmy that Highway 11 was his best bet: truckers preferred it for its lack of icy hills. And so Jimmy developed a plan to cope with the often sub-zero temperatures. Rather than stand at the side of the road turning blue and hypothermic, Jimmy would sit inside a truck stop at the Nipigon highway junction, drinking coffee and waiting for somebody to offer him a ride.

That was how one bitterly cold December afternoon, Jimmy met a trucker named Percy. When Percy saw the lonely hitchhiker sitting at a table drinking coffee, he mumbled gruffly at him and motioned for Jimmy to grab his backpack and hop on board. Jimmy couldn't have been more relieved. It was –35 degrees Celsius outside, and he'd already been waiting for several hours. His cheer soon faded, however, when just minutes down the road the effects of excessive coffee-drinking started building an undeniable and increasingly urgent pressure in his bladder.

"I'm sorry to tell you this," Jimmy admitted sheepishly, "but I've really gotta go to the bathroom. Can you pull the truck over?"

Percy gave him a perturbed look, mumbled something about ice on the road, and told Jimmy that he'd have to wait until Longlac.

How far they were from Longlac Jimmy couldn't remember, but after another few minutes he realized it was farther than he could wait. "Look man," he said finally, desperation creeping into his voice, "I know it was really irresponsible of me to drink so much coffee back there, but I gotta go!"

"We can't stop till Longlac," Percy said flatly.

Ten minutes of unspeakable agony passed, every jarring bump on the road forcing Jimmy closer to the edge. It wasn't long before he'd reached the point of no return. "Listen man," he pleaded, "I can't hold it any longer! Either you stop the truck or it's going on the floor!"

Percy looked at him coolly and repeated his mantra one last time. "I'm not stopping till Longlac, kid. If you've gotta go that badly, here's what you've gotta do."

A minute later, Jimmy opened his door, wrapped one arm around the truck's running bar, and stepped precariously onto the six-inch steel grate. Blasting along at 120 kilometres per hour in the middle of a Northern Ontario deep-freeze, he gingerly unzipped his fly, pulled out his equipment, and aimed for the ditch. When he clambered back into the truck a couple of minutes later—red-faced and shivering, ice crystals hanging from his hair—he found Percy doubled over the wheel laughing.

"You know, I've told a hundred hitchhikers to do that," Percy wheezed, trying to catch his breath. "But you're the first guy who ever did it!"

Matthew Jackson

Canmore, Alberta

ORANGE JUICE

Twenty years ago I worked as a waitress in a mediocre Italian restaurant in downtown Toronto. The restaurant was at the corner of Queen and Bathurst, which at the time was in the throes of an identity crisis—trying to trade in its back-alley image for a hipper, trendier look.

Between shifts at the restaurant I often killed time at Galaxy Donuts—a coffee shop that was home to the neighbourhood's castaways. The people I met in Galaxy Donuts were vulnerable, defensive, and streetwise. They were everything that I—a trusting twenty-year-old from small-town British Columbia—was not.

One morning as I sat with a coffee in front of me—more for the company than the caffeine—I heard a raspy voice behind me.

"Hey you!"

I squirmed in my chair.

"You!" the voice said again.

I turned and found myself looking into the hollow eyes of a woman whose life was the street. It was hard to guess her age. She might have been fifty; she could have been seventy. Her hair was shoulder-length, grey, and matted to her head. The contents of her life, rolled up in two canvas duffle bags, lay like faithful dogs at her feet.

"You got any red-haired girls?" the woman asked, staring at my own head of red hair.

"No," I replied.

The woman had opened one of her sacks and was rummaging for something.

"No," I repeated, "I don't have any kids."

But it didn't matter now—she hadn't heard me, it seemed. She was intent on digging something out of her bag. Relieved, I turned back to my coffee.

"Here," she said, handing me a small plastic doll. The doll was about six inches tall. Her cheeks were freckled and her hair was an outrageous shade of orange. Her name, according to the words printed on her speckled dress, was Orange Juice. The expression on her face gave her a perky, impish look.

"When you get a daughter, give 'er that," the woman said.

"Thanks," I said. "I will." I offered a smile to show that I was sincere, but by then the woman had turned away.

The little doll named Orange Juice followed me through the next decade of my life, to different cities, other provinces, even a new continent. Each time I packed up my possessions to set forth on another chapter of my life, I would take Orange Juice down from whichever shelf or tabletop had served as her perch and pack her in my bag. The cheery-faced, orange-haired doll that had once been a part of that woman's life was now a part of mine. There was something special in that.

A few years ago when my daughter became interested in dolls, she asked about the doll standing among her mother's perfume bottles and jewellery boxes. The time had come to fulfill the old woman's request. I removed the doll from my dresser top and placed it in the hands of my little red-haired girl.

The doll named Orange Juice has become a part of my daughter's life now, and the woman who had no home and no name, whose life seemed so detached from any other, has made one more small connection.

Barbara Olson

Nelson, British Columbia

RUNNING IN THE FAMILY

As a child, I loved the thrill of a good race. "I'll spot you half a block," my father would say, and I'd run like the dickens toward the stop sign at the corner of our street. That was our finish line. And it wasn't until I'd crossed the line that my father would catch up with me. It was exhilarating. I was just a kid, but I could always beat him.

Dad was a fabulous runner. He could jog smoothly for miles without showing any signs of fatigue, but sprinting was his specialty. He'd race me everywhere. He'd chase my sister and me through the empty lot that bordered our home. Duchess, our collie, often joined in the fun, circling round our feet.

During World War II, my father was a private in the Canadian Army. He was stationed in Petawawa, Ontario, just a few hours from my parents' apartment in Montreal. They were newlyweds and my mother never missed an opportunity to visit Dad at the base.

In his second year of service, the news came that my father was going to be shipped overseas to do a tour of duty. There was no time for anything more than a quick goodbye phone call. Dad travelled by train to Nova Scotia to meet the ship that would take him abroad.

The days in Nova Scotia were filled with organized activities and competitions to entertain the troops while they waited to ship out. My father ran "the mile," and to everyone's surprise, Dad wasn't just good—he was exceptional. So when the troop ship sailed to Europe a few days later, it left without my father. The army had decided to keep him in Canada to race competitively. Five months later he was discharged and returned home to Montreal, where he and my mother were reunited.

Years later, when I was a teenager, my father began to slow down. We ran together less often, and during our races he seemed to struggle. In his mid-forties he was diagnosed with Parkinson's disease. Dad was no longer the vibrant, energetic man I knew. Every movement became an effort, and although he was fiercely independent in spirit, his mobility deteriorated over the years and he often fell. Eventually, one of his falls left him with a serious injury and he was admitted to hospital. He never lived in our house again.

My father spent the last seven years of his life in a nursing home, strapped into a wheelchair. When there was no one to push him, my father's life literally came to a standstill.

Shortly after my father died I began running regularly, usually with friends. I entered my first race since high school days. It was a fundraiser for a women's shelter and I was proud to run for the cause. Next, I participated in a race to support breast cancer research. In no time, I was racing regularly to support worthy causes.

I've run dozens of races in the ten years since Dad's death. This year I ran my third Boston Marathon.

I'm proud of my accomplishments as a runner. I'm only sorry that my father never had the opportunity to share these moments with me. I think of my dad every race I run. As I push myself through the miles, I think of the struggles he endured courageously over so many years. I think about the man, once agile and fit, and the cruel fate to which he fell victim.

But mostly, I think about our countless races down the block, so many years ago, and how he always let me win.

Deena Sacks

Hamilton, Ontario

MEASURE OF A DOG

I'm a blind person and I use a guide dog. A number of years ago I was working as a secretary in a large building. My guide dog, Trixie, guided me to work and around the office. Trixie was a black Labrador retriever, and like most Labs, loved to carry things in her mouth. The women in the office had given Trixie an old twelve-inch wooden ruler to play with, and she loved it so much that she insisted on carrying it everywhere we went.

One day Trixie and I were walking along the corridor in the office building. We came to a double fire door, of which only one half was open. Two men stood there chatting as we passed. Trixie, as usual, was carrying her ruler in her mouth and she carefully negotiated her way past the two men and through the fire door.

As we continued down the corridor, I heard one of the men remark, "Did you see the way that dog measured the doorway to see if there was enough room for both of them to get through?"

Margaret Thomson
St. John's, Newfoundland and Labrador

THE OUTHOUSE

The outhouse at our cottage was like most outdoor toilets at cottages all across Canada. It was painted bright white to give the impression of being clean and sanitary. But this outhouse had something different hidden within. Instead of a hole in the ground beneath the seat, our outhouse had an empty forty-five-gallon drum. The drum was to be removed and emptied when full—eliminating the hassle of relocating the building and digging a new hole when the old one became full.

This idea was my father's brainchild.

After mental calculations—which I'm sure involved Einstein's theory of relativity, chaos theory, and quantum physics—Dad figured that the drum would take at least two years to fill.

One weekend we headed up north to the cottage and discovered that Dad had erred in his calculations. It had been just two months since he'd installed the tank, but it was already overflowing. We had horrifying visions of bailing out the contents of the barrel, but much to our surprise Dad said this wouldn't be necessary. He said everything was "under control."

Now, when Dad was discharged from the army at the end of the Second World War, he was permitted to retain his Lee Enfield 303 rifle. For what purpose I'm not sure, unless his commanders foresaw the dilemma that was to befall him in the summer of 1960.

I had never known Dad to use a rifle. So when I saw him working the bolt action and inserting a shell into the chamber, I was intrigued. (I was an eleven-year-old boy; anything that involved guns was interesting.) My mother and my three brothers and I gathered on the porch and watched as Dad made his way, weapon in hand, to the small white building in the bush.

Dad's plan was to puncture the barrel in several strategic places, permitting the liquid portion of the contents to drain away. According to his new calculations, this remedy would permit us to use the system until next summer.

By this time we'd gathered near the front of the outhouse to watch his act of genius. Dad entered the building, lifted the seat, and brought the weapon to his shoulder. Just as he was about to squeeze the trigger a gust of wind swung the outhouse door closed, engulfing him in darkness.

The 303's report was strong enough to rattle the door on its hinges, but it didn't open until Dad pushed it from the inside.

He staggered out of the tiny building with his hands covering his ears, moaning something about a ringing sound and a stinging in his eyes.

He was covered head to toe.

None of us had the courage to go near Dad; in fact we all backed away as he lurched—stunned and stinking—around in the bush. Mom, who had to yell to be heard above the ringing in Dad's ears, directed him to the lake where he removed his clothing and washed.

The outhouse, which had been plastered with artwork and pink newspaper clippings, was ruined. The pink *Toronto Telegram* pages were no longer pink. A major refit was in order—a job eventually assigned to Dad.

We ended up moving the outhouse the next weekend, and Dad never tried shooting in enclosed spaces again. As a matter of fact, I don't think Dad fired a rifle for the rest of his life.

Willy Mehew

Calgary, Alberta

(submitted by his mom, Gladys Sandland of Newcastle, Ontario)

LOVINGLY MADE
BY GRANDMA

It was September 1997 and I was two weeks away from delivering our first child. It was nearly seven years to the day that we'd lost my mom to a breakdown and suicide. The shock, denial, grief, and anger had been pretty much worked through and accepted. What remained was the sadness of knowing that my mom would never see the grandchild she had yearned for.

Two days before my baby shower my sister came over with our stepmother, Mary. We'd resented Mary when she first entered our lives, but that resentment had turned into appreciation and, eventually, to love.

Mary handed me a gift bag. Reaching in past the ribbons and tissue paper, I was surprised to feel something woolly. Mary was a master seamstress, yet I'd never known her to knit before. The tag read, "Lovingly made by Grandma."

"Wow Mary, I didn't know you could knit too!" I said, admiring the dainty newborn coats.

Mary became teary. She explained that when she'd moved in with my dad, six years earlier, she'd come across my mom's knitting bag. Inside were the two tiny coats she'd been working on before she died. Mary had been saving the coats for me all these years.

Two days later at my baby shower I proudly related the story of how Mary—of all people—had saved a little piece of my mom for me.

The last gift that day came from Colleen—my mom's best friend's daughter. I read Colleen's card aloud: "Leslie, everything in this basket, including the basket, was given to me by your mother at my own baby shower ten years ago."

As I held up the various infant ensembles for everyone to see, there wasn't a dry eye in the house. It was lovely to be reminded of my mom's generosity. We all remembered her that day with fondness and laughter, rather than the grief that had gripped us at the time of her death. She touched others who, in turn, waited years to touch me.

Leslie Walsh
Aurora, Ontario

SUMMERLAND

Sunday was always Pancake Day at our house. Mom prepared her pancake batter from scratch, while my younger brother grated cheddar cheese and I beat the eggs for the cheese omelettes. Everyone got their own tri-folded, two-egg cheese omelette to accompany their pancakes.

Once the cast-iron skillets were hot enough, I ladled out the first batch of pancakes. Dad read the paper in the living room. He'd save much of Saturday's *Globe and Mail* for Sunday morning, keeping abreast of stocks and options and Parliament and Moscow and the situation in the Middle East—there was always a situation in the Middle East. Both my parents had emigrated from Egypt in the 1960s, largely to elude its proneness to "situations."

When the first batch of pancakes was ready, I'd serve myself and my brother, and then abandon my post. Dad got the second batch. Mom continued preparing pancakes and cheese omelettes as fast as we could consume them. Only when the last batch was done would she sit and join us. Then Dad would regale the family with stories from the world of science, of his job at the technical college, of the political arena, or of a genre I can only describe as modern fairy tales. Like the one about the fireman emerging from the burning mansion clutching what turned out to be a beautiful, lifelike doll in a jumble of swaddling, while the doll's greedy, petulant owner remained trapped inside.

Around our Sunday morning breakfast table, I heard about the Doppler effect and the tissue plasminogen activator years before I heard about them in school. And I devoured the tales as earnestly as the pancakes.

In fact, I used to gobble up the blurbs on any product placed on the kitchen table. As a result of Canada's language laws, I am proud to say that I remain fluently bilingual on the subjects of cereal, milk, and contest sweepstakes.

Most Sundays I favoured Aunt Jemima's table syrup. On some occasions, however, a flask-shaped bottle with shoulders and a bulbous neck appeared on the table. It was filled with berry or peach syrup that made your knees buckle. The label said it was made by a company called Summerland Sweets.

The syrup bottle said the exquisite nectar came from Summerland, British Columbia. It seemed a magical place to me as a child. A place where the sun shone bright and hot. Where you could wake up, wander out to your very own peach tree, pick a fist-sized peach, and bite into its glistening flesh, warmed by the morning sun. It seemed about as far away from Edmonton, where I was born and raised, as I could imagine. As I grew into an adolescent, I continued to believe the place was fictitious, and scoffed at the Pollyanna whose unchecked optimism could have named a company—let alone a place—"Summerland."

More than a decade later, I am now the patriarch of my own young family. On Sundays, my sons get the first batch, my wife gets the second, and I don't abandon my post at the Teflon skillets anymore. I've discovered maple syrup. My five-year-old, Denzel, laps up anything he can read within the range of his sharp eyes and keener mind, including cereal boxes. Theo, his younger brother, sticks to the pancakes, omelette, and conversation. Sometimes, the food sticks to him.

Today, my wife, Janet, brought a flask of Summerland Sweets Black & Raspberry Syrup to the table, and I smiled as I dribbled it over my pancakes. And, in light of what I now know, I shook my head at the naïveté of my childhood and the arrogance of my adolescence. Summerland is real. In fact, Summerland is forty kilometres from where we live, just beyond the similarly improbably named Peachland. We moved to the arid Okanagan Valley nearly two years ago. We live among orchards and vineyards, irrigated oases among the grass and scrub. Of course, the sun is blazing as I write this.

My favourite time of year is August, when I can walk out my front door and pick a fist-sized peach from my very own peach tree. Somebody pinch me. On second thought, don't.

Islam Mohamed

Kelowna, British Columbia

YEAR
TWO

MR. FISHER

When I was going to high school I had the good fortune to have Mr. Fisher for grade eleven history. The class was "People and Politics," a history of the twentieth century. Mr. Fisher used to be a boxer and he moved around his classroom the way a boxer dances around his ring.

I'd heard stories about Mr. Fisher and his history class. I'd heard that during his description of Vimy Ridge he got up on his desk and *rat-a-tat-tatted* an imagined machine gun at the students in their desks. I'd heard that Mr. Fisher waved around a blue handkerchief. To say the least, I was curious.

During our first week, Mr. Fisher taught us the basics of how he wanted assignments handed in. We were to underline the date, title, and our name with a red pen, and we were to use a ruler. Our writing was to be legible, or assignments would be handed back. I saw a few people get papers handed back for poor penmanship. Mr. Fisher did not fool around.

During our study of World War I, Mr. Fisher made the trenches imaginable for us. We were stunned and horrified by what we learned. He explained the tragedies of a soldier's suffering with tears streaming down his face, his big blue handkerchief always at the ready. We were learning, and learning well.

There was a boy named Dennis who sat in front of me in Mr. Fisher's neatly ordered rows. Dennis was a troublemaker. Dennis often had his assignments handed back to him. Dennis was often late for class. In Mr. Fisher's world, lateness was not acceptable. One day, in the middle of term, Dennis came in late and sat down after tossing his assignment onto Mr. Fisher's desk. Mr. Fisher had reached his boiling point. He stood up, pushed back his chair, grabbed Dennis's paper, ripped it in half, and threw it into the garbage can. He rushed over to Dennis's desk, pointed his finger in his face, and began a two-minute tirade. He berated Dennis for everything from his tardiness to his messy hair. The whole class was uncomfortable. The longer the tirade continued, the quieter the room got. And Dennis never said a thing. He didn't even look up at Mr. Fisher.

Suddenly, Mr. Fisher stopped, patted Dennis on the shoulder, and said "Thank you, Dennis."

Then Mr. Fisher turned his eyes on us. "I stood here for two minutes completely humiliating this boy in front of all of you, and not one of you said anything. You all knew I was out of line, and had no right to be saying those things to Dennis, yet nobody tried to stop me. Why? Because I'm a teacher, a figure of authority? Because you were afraid?"

Not one of us could meet his gaze, so he continued, "Dennis was expecting this today, because I asked him to come in late and throw his homework on my desk. I asked his permission to rant at him like a lunatic for a couple of minutes."

All of us looked up at Mr. Fisher and Dennis, mouths agape.

"Today," he said, "we begin our study of the Holocaust, the Second World War, and how it started."

There are not many things that I remember about grade eleven. I don't remember how to do polynomial equations anymore, and I'm not sure how to conjugate the past participle of a female pronoun in French. But as long as I live, I will never forget that morning in Mr. Fisher's class.

Yes, he was eccentric, and yes, he did get up on his desk and re-enact gun battles from the First World War. But he also celebrated with us when Nelson Mandela was let out of prison, and wept as he read the article detailing Mandela's first hours of freedom. He used his blue handkerchief to blow his nose, mop his brow, and always, to wipe his tears. Mr. Fisher taught us to be accountable, to be empathetic, and not to be afraid to stand up when we knew something wasn't right. In the four months that I had him as a teacher, I grew to love him like a father. I can only hope that more children have a Mr. Fisher in their lives.

Irene Wood

Edmonton, Alberta

FATSO, THE CAT

When we were first married we lived in a small but comfortable two-storey house. We shared our house with three cats. If you understand cats, then you know that in reality they deigned to share the house with us.

The lone male cat was an impressive black-and-tan tabby with huge white paws and an expansive white belly. He tipped the scales at roughly twenty-three pounds. We'd named him Screech because he had a plaintive, wailing meow. But he was more commonly known, to me anyway, as Fatso. Screech was in the habit of sleeping on his back with his back legs sprawled and his front paws held aloft. We often came across him in this position lying in a sunbeam, his massive white belly shimmering in the sunlight.

At the back of our house we had a detached garage. As you walked down the back steps and sidewalk on the way to the garage you got a good view of the neighbours' backyard and deck.

The neighbour lady was in the habit of gardening and suntanning in a bikini that she had, regrettably, vastly outgrown.

One hot weekend morning as I left to run some errands,

I came out the back door to see Screech sprawled paws up and belly exposed to the sun. In a loud voice filled with affection I hollered out, "Sunning your belly, Fatso?"

Three strides farther down the sidewalk, I caught sight of our neighbour hastily refastening her bikini and struggling to her feet from her suntanning position on her deck. She shot me a look that almost reduced me to tears.

Trying to cover my tracks, I made a big production out of greeting the cat and playing with him. He stalked off, tail held high, his dignity intact as I slunk into the garage and drove away.

I never did find out if our neighbour understood that I was talking to Fatso the cat and not her. Needless to say it was some time before we spoke again.

Tony and Maureen Smith
Calgary, Alberta

I TOLD YOU SO

It was Thanksgiving. I met my mother at her home in Chatham and then we headed to our cottage for the holiday weekend.

Along the way we made an unscheduled stop at Jack Miner's Bird Sanctuary. Mom had grown up in southwestern Ontario and had often regaled me with stories of the Canada geese that stopped there during migration. The fields, she said, were "black with birds." Why we decided to stop this year I don't remember, but we did. It wasn't like we did it often, and in fact, we haven't done it since. I remember thinking it wasn't worth stopping.

When we did stop it was apparent that the migration had begun. The field set aside for the birds was already full.

On the edge of the field there was an old-fashioned blackboard, on which someone had written that the geese would arrive daily at 4:00 and 4:25 p.m. Yeah right, I thought. I mean really, how could they know the time? I doubted that any birds would arrive at all.

Well, it was nearly 4:00 p.m. so I told Mom we might as well hang around to see what happened. I remember she smiled, a little smugly I might add, knowing full well what was to happen. We were in the midst of swans and mallards when I noticed a peculiar sound.

Out of the east, from the direction of Leamington, the geese came flying in. They came in by the hundreds, if not thousands, and they descended onto the field just across the road. On and on they came, a seemingly endless stream of geese, flapping and squawking as only geese can do, so loud you couldn't hear yourself think.

I stood for a moment, stock-still and stunned. I couldn't believe the sheer number! When I got over my initial shock, I checked my watch.

My jaw dropped.

4:00 p.m.

Not a minute before or after, but bang on the hour!

The geese continued to fly in for several more minutes. I was beginning to wonder if there'd be an end to them. Eventually there were just a few geese in the sky. Most of the hundreds had landed on what was now a very full field. I'd just caught my breath when, wouldn't you know, the whole thing started up again.

This time the birds came in from the direction of Essex. I checked my watch, and yup, you guessed it, it was precisely 4:25 p.m. I remember thinking that if the buses in Toronto were as punctual as those two flocks of birds, my daily commute would be far less painful.

I still feel awestruck by what I saw that day in late October so many years ago. By that, and by the fact that my mom never said "I told you so" even though she had every right to.

Bethanne O'Neil

Edmonton, Alberta

HOW TO BE
A BETTER MAN

My wife, Helen, and I were in love. We had two beautiful daughters—three years and twelve months old—and I'd just returned from my third peacekeeping tour in Bosnia. The reunions are the best part of the tours. You get the opportunity to fall in love with your partner again. Six months of separation causes immense emotion. The plane ride home is long and filled with intense anticipation. The joy of that first hug is magic. This reunion was further blessed with the knowledge that Helen was pregnant. We had no worries.

Life can change quickly. Three months later the ultrasound technician asked us if we had a history of twins in the family. In shock, we learned that Helen would give birth to a girl and a boy—Sofia and Connor.

After the birth we quickly realized that the work was extreme. The twins' routine was exhausting. My career had evolved and I was busier. Work was stressful and I was falling behind. And now Helen had four children competing for her attention. We both became irritable. We had no time together to make things right again. There was no time for anything but the children.

I dreaded the late-night feedings and came to fear the way I felt about the twins. When I came home from Bosnia I'd been looking forward to reconnecting with my wife. But Helen was absorbed with caring for the children. This made me feel even more isolated. She didn't seem worried about our loss of our intimacy. I felt guilty and selfish. I felt useless.

Helen and I began to argue about little things—things that weren't important. I lost my cool a few times when it was my turn to feed the children. I blamed it on work, but it was more than that. I'd spend the next day shamed by my lack of strength and wondering whether or not I really wanted to keep going down this road.

One night I arrived home tired and unhappy after a particularly bad day at work. One of the twins, Sofia, was sick. She woke up crying around four in the morning. Helen was exhausted and I knew she needed more sleep. So I scooped Sofia up from her crib and sat on a wicker chair in the nursery, rocking my crying child and thinking about how I was feeling. I felt like a failure. I wanted time to myself. I wanted it to be like it was four months ago. For the first time in my life I seriously considered quitting. I'm no good as a father, I thought. I wanted out. I wanted to throw my crying child down and run away.

And just then I realized the crying had stopped. In the low light I looked down at my baby daughter, and—I will never forget this moment—right then my sick, helpless daughter looked up at me and did something she'd never done before. She smiled. The first smile of her life, given to me as a gift when I needed it the most.

I cried and cried, and my tears fell on her face. But she wouldn't stop smiling at me. I held her tight.

I slept in that chair all night with Sofia. In the morning I laid her back in her crib and snuck into my children's rooms to kiss them and silently tell them I loved them. I walked outside and took a breath of the fresh morning air.

It took me a long time to share this story with my wife. The next time I tell it aloud, it will be to my daughter. And when I do, I'll be thanking her for making me a better man.

Phil Millar

London, Ontario

THE FIREMAN

My son Luke loved firefighters as a boy. He also loved costumes. Over the years Luke dressed up as all the well-known super-heroes—Superman, Batman, Spider-Man—as well as some of the lesser known characters. Characters, I learned later, that were a figment of his imagination. I helped Luke make super-hero costumes: we sewed onion bags on his coat sleeves for Spider-Man, attached capes to his clothing, and cut out letters to attach to his T-shirts. The neighbours loved it.

His favourite alter ego was "Fireman." He wore an old navy jacket of mine that reached his knees, his fireman hat, and his Wellington boots. And he always brought along his trusty fire truck with the extension ladder. We even constructed a fire hose out of wool and foil. At the park Luke would play on the climber, slide down the fire pole, drive his truck to the scene of the fire, and then save the day with his fire hose.

One day, while we were playing, we heard the sound of a real fire engine. We lived in a big city at the time, so that wasn't uncommon, but on this particular day the truck came down the street and past the park. We watched it whiz past and then stop suddenly in front of an apartment building that was billowing smoke. It was very exciting.

Luke quickly grabbed his own fire engine and took off down the street. By the time we got on the scene the firefighters had the blaze under control.

As I watched the action, I became aware of Luke setting up his truck and taking his hose out of his pocket. Just then a firefighter, who I guess had noticed this small boy dressed as a fireman complete with wool hose and miniature fire truck, came over and said to him, "Come on, let's go, we've got a fire to fight!"

Luke looked at him, in shock, and said, "I'm not the real Fireman, I'm just a small boy."

Allison West Armstrong

Arnprior, Ontario

FADED LOVE

I've forgotten whether Mireille's room was on the sixth or seventh floor of the ancient walk-up apartment building at 7 rue St. Martin. It doesn't matter. She was a small Norman woman from Urville-Bocage, but I met her in Paris in 1970.

Mireille's single room served as a kitchen, living room, and bedroom. The loo was in the hall. Beneath her bed she kept a large stone crock of cherries soaked in calvados, the fiery distilled apple spirits of her native Normandy.

Our actual acquaintance was brief: a month in the summer, and another in December of 1970. George Harrison's "My Sweet Lord" was topping the charts, and Mireille, who was nine years my senior, called me "My Sweet Lord" and "Robert, you clever boy." Truth to say, in 1970, I was, in many ways, still a boy.

Mireille cooked splendid French meals for me on a tiny hot plate, and through the small dormer window of her room, pointed out the hermaphrodite gargoyle on the cathedral across the street. That was the year it snowed in Paris before Christmas, pure white flakes the size of silver dollars dissolving like fallen angels into the black waters of the Seine. Mireille asked me not to leave for North America before Christmas, but I did. I took a cab to Orly on Christmas Eve, and flew to New York on an almost empty 747.

She wrote me many love letters, and I wrote back. She asked me to come live with her on her father's farm in Normandy and raise "a half a dozen of cows." In one letter, written from that farm, she enclosed a pressed violet.

At the end of 1996, which had been a singularly loveless year for me, I busied myself moving old papers around my apartment in a vain effort to convince myself that I was actually accomplishing something. I came upon Mireille's letters, and reread them all again. It had been more than ten years since I'd last looked at them. They were poignant and touching and made me feel the fool, or much worse, for having rejected her love. At last, as I knew that I must, I came to the letter containing the flower. Perhaps I shouldn't have been surprised that it had faded so. But I was surprised by how little of the indigo summer of twenty-five years ago remained.

Bob Friedland

Richmond, British Columbia

FROM FATHER, FINALLY

I was at an antiques show in Abbotsford, British Columbia.

I was wandering around the fairgrounds looking at the odds and ends when I suddenly said to my friend, "That's my father!" We were looking at a wartime picture. The face, my father's, was a real photograph and the body was a cartoon drawing of a man strutting with his chest stuck out to show his new rank. In the lower left corner was my father's nickname, on the epaulet was "PPCLI," and in the lower right corner was an inscription: "To Alan from Daddy with love, Christmas 1942." My father had known my brother for about a year before he was called up to fight. He had never known me.

My mother and father were divorced after the war. Dad married a nurse from Winnipeg whom he'd met after being invalided out of the Sicilian campaign. In 1944 our mother sold off the family farm near Georgetown and moved back to her hometown of London. She must have cleared out Father's memorabilia and given it to his relatives near Limehouse. We never heard from Father again.

I bought the photo, packed it up, and sent it to my brother.

It was the first time he'd seen it in fifty-nine years. It was of particular interest to him as he's had several strokes and is sometimes more interested in the past than in the present.

It was a special moment, finding that photo, and I'm so grateful to have found this new, and only, memory of our father.

Ann Sutherland

White Rock, British Columbia

CANADIAN TIRES

I was born in Arvida, Quebec, in March, 1959. My father, an Alcan man, was transferred to Riverside, California, in 1966.

On a fine March day when I was in grade eleven, five friends and I left Riverside in my buddy Brad's Plymouth Fury II. We were heading for the San Bernardino Mountains. We wanted to "go to the snow"; it was spring break and we loved to toboggan. The mountains of the Cajon Pass can be full of interesting surprises. Most of them having to do with the weather.

The car was typical of a high school kid's car. We had just enough gas to get home and all four tires were of different makes, though equally bald. Between the six of us we had about $1.85 in loose coins.

When we arrived in the mountains at mid-morning it was sunny and clear. At about noon, however, it began to snow: big, fat flakes that floated down slowly and stuck to the stuff that was already there. Throughout the day, the rate at which the snow was falling steadily picked up. I mentioned this to Brad and he said, "Don't worry about it, we'll be fine." So, we kept tobogganing.

The snow got deeper.

After a couple of hours and maybe eight to ten inches of fresh snow, Brad decided we should leave before the California Highway Patrol closed the Cajon Pass. He handed me the keys to his pride and joy and said, "Here, you drive. And if the cops ask any questions, let me do the talking."

We piled into his Fury II and away we went, only to be stopped by the long line of cars heading to the highway on-ramp.

The Highway Patrol had the on-ramp blocked. They were turning cars away. We crept forward slowly. It kept snowing.

As we got closer we could see that the highway—all four lanes leading back to Riverside and all four lanes going in the opposite direction—was fresh, white, and pristine. There wasn't a mark on it.

After half an hour of inching forward, we made it to the road block at the on-ramp. I rolled down the window and some snow blew in, followed by a cop's head. The cop's head said, "Where are you boys going?"

Brad leaned forward and said, "Sir, we're going back to Riverside."

The cop looked at me and said, "The Cajon Pass is closed because there are ten to twelve inches of fresh powder on it. You have a two-hour wait until the plow arrives and you'll need chains on those tires."

Brad leaned forward again and said to the cop, "Yes, sir." Then he pointed at me and said, "He's Canadian."

The cop looked at me—in awe—and said, "Are you really *Canadian*?"

"Yes sir, I was born in Quebec," I said. I wasn't really sure what this was all about.

The cop pulled his head out of our car, turned to the other officers, and said, "It's okay, this one can go through. There's a Canadian driving."

They stepped aside and away we went. And we drove home without incident.

Ian D. Haynes
Windsor, Ontario

THE CELLO

On Easter Monday my family's life came to an abrupt halt. My daughter and son-in-law's first baby was stillborn. It was such a shocking, devastating event. All the hopes and dreams of a new generation, all the expected joy of arrival, now turned into the grief of departure. I flew to Toronto to be with them and was overwhelmed by the outpouring of love and support from family and friends, many of whom had travelled long distances to attend the funeral of a little girl they'd never had the chance to know.

During the days that followed the funeral, we spent a lot of time talking about life and death, trying to make some sense of the purpose behind this loss. My granddaughter was named Strummer, after the musician Joe Strummer who also died before his time. In lieu of flowers, my daughter and son-in-law requested that trees—red maples—be donated to the Joe Strummer Memorial Forest on the Isle of Skye in Scotland.

This was a wonderful idea, but I wanted to do something to memorialize Strummer's death that was more personal to me. Alone at night in my hotel room, I thought about what I could do that would help me turn a little girl's death into something positive. People are communicators. We use words, movement, art, and music to tell our stories. This is what makes us human.

On Monday morning I walked through the door of Heinl's music store. A young man approached and asked if he could be of help, and I replied, "Yes, I'd like to buy a cello." I knew nothing about cellos and had never played one, but it had always been in the back of my mind that I'd like to try. A used one had just arrived at the music store. I was quoted a price and told it could be shipped to Nova Scotia. I said that I'd think about it. I phoned the next day and bought the cello. And not long after, I found a wonderful music teacher who's helped me learn to play.

I never had the chance to hold my granddaughter or to hear her laugh, but when I pick up my cello and hold it close to me, when I pull the bow across the strings and attempt to play the music of many generations gone by, I feel that the little girl left me a great and wonderful gift. It led me out of great sorrow and into a world full of song and hope.

Betsy Miller

Granville Ferry, Nova Scotia

THE CHRISTMAS TRAIN

One of the most treasured moments of my life happened on a night train bound for Thunder Bay from Sudbury. It was Christmas, sometime in the late 1970s.

Three of us, all sister teachers, were going to visit a family at the lakehead for part of the Christmas holiday. We boarded the train at 10:25 p.m., on December 25.

It was one of those perfect winter nights—crisp, cold air, crunchy snow, lots of stars, and a bright, bitten-cookie of a moon shining down on us as we pulled out of the Sudbury station. The train wasn't full. I wondered about the people who shared our car—alone on Christmas Day. I'm sure they wondered about us, too.

The car was calm and quiet. We passed Levack and Cartier, where the dark pines heavy with snow were Christmas card cutouts. It was beautiful.

Just as I rested my head and closed my eyes, something wonderful happened. In the dark, a clear voice began to sing "Silent Night." One by one other voices joined in.

When "Silent Night" was finished someone else started

another song, and then another and another after that. Not a word was spoken as one Christmas carol after another rang out—no stumbling over words, or hesitation, or even discussion as to what to sing next—the music just poured out spontaneously. Each of us taking part.

There was no comment or applause. The singing ended with one solo performance—from a darkened seat in the middle of the car—something from Handel's *Messiah*. It was past midnight as quiet descended and people drifted off to sleep.

I can't remember now which part of the *Messiah* closed that impromptu concert, but I'm reminded of that magical night each Christmas. The passengers in that car shared the unexpected gift of the joy and peace of that first holy night and, by the end, we were no longer strangers.

Sister Irina Bottos

Blind River, Ontario

YEAR
THREE

PLACEBO

When I was in college, back in the sixties, I worked part-time in a drugstore in Warren, Michigan.

One day we received a telephone call from the doctor at a nearby clinic. The doctor asked if we could still compound prescriptions. Although most drugstore pharmacists count pills from larger bottles into small plastic vials, they would—on occasion—have to mix a compound as directed by a physician. I don't know if druggists still do this, but they did back then.

So when the doctor asked if we could do it, I said sure.

"I have this patient," he said, "and he's been to every doctor I know. He complains about everything, but there's nothing wrong with him. He's a hypochondriac. Here's what I want you to do. Take the largest empty capsules you have and fill them with sugar. Make up ten of these capsules. Tell my patient that it's the most powerful painkiller ever devised. Tell him you can't even tell him the name of the pill, because it's experimental. Tell him the ingredients are secret. Tell him it's so powerful that he can take only one a day. Tell him that it's a narcotic. Tell him it's highly addictive. Tell him that it's so addictive that he can never, ever get a refill. Tell him whatever you want—just so he believes it ... Oh," added the doctor, "charge him a lot, or else he won't think it's any good."

Richard, the night pharmacist, gleefully filled the prescription. He stuck one of every warning label we had on the small bottle. He put two of the bright red skull-and-crossbones "DANGER" stickers on it.

When the customer arrived, Richard took him aside and gravely counselled him on the horribleness and extreme potency of this medication. He gave him explicit instructions not to drive after taking it, not to operate machinery, not to go out in the sun, not to do just about anything.

Sure enough, ten days later the customer called, declaring the sugar-filled capsules the best thing that had ever happened to him.

And although he did beg for a refill, or even just *one* more of the miracle pills, Richard had to apologize and tell him that, according to the law, we couldn't do that.

Jeff Aisen
Huntington Woods, Michigan

DRIVE-THROUGH RAINBOW

My family decided to celebrate Thanksgiving weekend in a cabin on a lake, not far from our home. My husband and I left on Friday afternoon, a little earlier than the rest of the family, so that we could open the cabin and get organized before they arrived.

The weather was *interesting*.

We drove through rainy patches of road and sunny patches of road. Then, all of a sudden, the windshield misted over and there was a brilliant white light filled with coloured spectrums. The colours were more intense than any I had ever seen. It lasted about fifteen seconds. The speed limit was ninety kilometres an hour and I prayed that the road ahead was straight, because I couldn't see anything else. It was a bit scary. But I kept telling myself that maybe there'd be a pot of gold under the hood when we arrived at the cabin.

Alas, there wasn't. But we'd been granted an unusual life experience; I suspect my husband and I are the only people to have driven through the base of a rainbow.

Betty McIntosh
Westbank, British Columbia

FAMILY TIES

In 1945 my father-in-law, Harvey Botham, was twenty-four years old. It was the tail end of World War II, and Harvey was among the last of the Canadian liberating forces in France to depart for home. One blistering summer day Harvey and a pal were resting on a Lilles street corner when they were approached by a young French boy.

The boy, Stéphane, was able to communicate with gestures, a little English, and a friendly tug that he had a meal for the two soldiers. They followed him to the humble apartment of his parents, M. and Mme. Hancart.

The meal was marvellous. The conversation, however, was stilted. They spoke little French, and their hosts little English, but most importantly, the boys felt an appreciation for the work the Canadians had done. A bond was forged. Harvey returned to the Hancarts' home several times before he shipped back to Canada. They exchanged addresses but there was little communication ... until 1971.

In 1971 Harvey, now in his fifties, had a family of his own in North Vancouver.

Harvey's nineteen-year-old daughter, Lynn (my wife), had

been bitten by the wanderlust of youth and had set off to hitch-hike with a backpack across Europe. As she was preparing to go her dad said, "Why don't you look these people up? They were very nice to me twenty-six years ago."

To get her dad "off her back," she reluctantly took the address. Lynn was hoping, however, that her trip wouldn't involve any kind of social meeting with people of her father's generation. She was a teenager, getting *away* from old fogies, not trying to be *with* them.

Halfway through her trip Lynn reconsidered; she was eager to see a friendly face. She nervously called the phone number her father had given her. There was some initial confusion with the English and French, but a gracious Mme. Hancart once again hosted a tired and hungry Canadian. She prepared a wonderful meal, but like the first time, what was more important was the connection. Lynn departed the house with a promise to Mme. Hancart to look up her son, the young boy Stéphane, who had moved to Cannes.

Arriving in Cannes after a sweaty journey via nights in gritty hostels, Lynn placed a call to Stéphane's house. She was told to wait where she was. Moments later, a chauffeured car arrived, and Lynn was whisked to Stéphane's estate overlooking the Mediterranean, where he and his wife, Marie-Josée, treated Lynn like a queen for a week. The neighbours and relatives came over. There was wine and dancing and singing every night. It was the visit of a lifetime for my wife.

Fast-forward to 2002. Our daughter, twenty-two-year-old Rhoslyn, was backpacking from the Czech Republic to the South of France with a friend. Feeling tired and low, the girls called home.

"Why don't you call these people, the Hancarts? They're really nice," said Lynn. Suffice to say my daughter had the same feelings her mother had had, thirty-one years earlier.

But by the time they reached Cannes, broke and rundown, they too had changed their minds. They made a call in broken French to Stéphane's house. *"Mon grand-père est Harvey Botham,"* said Rhoslyn.

"Reste là!" said Stéphane. *"J'arriverai."*

Moments later, the chauffeur came down. Back to the estate they went. Neighbours came again. Wine and song and dance, every night for a week. Rhoslyn had the visit of a lifetime, just as her mother had so many years before.

Now, sixty-one years after that initial meeting in Lilles, Harvey is eighty-five. His relationship with Stéphane's family has grown with these post-war meetings, with numerous visits, bottles of wine, and acts of kindness and hospitality.

It's a relationship that has blossomed from a sacrifice that many young Canadians made decades ago, far from home, as their lives lay before them. I'm thankful they did.

Bryn Jones
Aldergrove, British Columbia

TE QUIERO MUCHO

I was born and raised in Mexico City. A hyper-hectic and dangerous corner of the world. Nine years ago, I travelled for the first time outside of Mexico as part of a student exchange program. It's easy to understand how culture-shocked I was when I arrived at my foster home in the coastal community of Botwood, Newfoundland: my hometown has a population of twenty million residents, and Botwood, buried between the wild boreal forest and the rough Atlantic Ocean, had a population about the same as my high school. It was, in almost every way, the complete opposite of my home.

Back then I didn't speak much English, and after listening to the thick, almost incomprehensible accent of the Botwood locals, I thought, "Oh boy, it's going to be a long summer."

Although I didn't know anybody in town, the news of the newly arrived Mexican student spread so fast that before I had the chance to finish unpacking I received my first invitation, from complete strangers, to join them for a cup of tea. The invitation came from Wally and his wife, Maria.

Wally and Maria were from Ecuador and spoke to me in Spanish when I really needed it. It was Wally and Maria who told me to go to the waterfront and hike the trail on the peninsula.

The next day I went down to the waterfront and hiked the peninsula and found a series of man-made caves. They were abandoned military refuges from the war. The caves were dark, hidden, private places, surrounded by thick, bomb-proof concrete walls. It was the absolute perfect place to practise my recently purchased flute.

A few weeks later, while in one of the caves, I got an unexpected visit from the local bike gang, about fifteen kids on bicycles ranging in age from nine to thirteen. They were all staring at me as if they'd never seen a Mexican flute player practising in a cave before.

They came in and asked me all kinds of questions, starting with, "Where are you from?" Followed by more challenging questions like, "Is it true that if I rob a bank I should go to Mexico because police will never find me there?" and "Can you play any Guns N' Roses on that flute?"

After five or ten minutes of questions they got back on their bikes and took off. Five seconds later the smallest kid came back. "I have one last question!" he said. "How do you say 'piss off' in Spanish?"

I peered at him and asked, "How old are you?"

"Nine," he replied. So I told the kid, "'Piss off' in Spanish is *Te quiero mucho.*"

"*Te quiero mucho?*" he repeated.

"Yes," I said. "Perfect."

Off he went on his bike, not having a clue that he'd just learned how to say "I love you so much" in Spanish.

I didn't realize what I'd done until the next morning when Wally and Maria's daughter phoned and told me that every single kid in Botwood between ages seven and fifteen was openly, verbally, and rather aggressively loving each other. In Spanish!

I went back to Mexico shortly after that. I haven't been back to Botwood since. But my time in Newfoundland fundamentally changed the way I see things: it doesn't matter how tough, how rough, or how cold it gets, Newfoundlanders always make it possible to view life in a positive, friendly, and warm manner. And I'm happy to tell you that tomorrow, at last, I'll be submitting my application for permanent residency in Canada.

I will finally be an authentic Mexicanadian.

Diego Ibarra

Mexico City, Mexico
(and now Halifax, Nova Scotia)

AMAZING GRACE

A few years ago a guy came to my door with a small present: a box of chocolate cookies and an empty travel mug.

"This is for you," he said. Then he asked if he could come in.

"I have a story to tell you," he said. "It goes back five hundred days."

Now, I play the bagpipes and sometimes people will give me a gift after I've played at a function, usually because the sound of the pipes touched them more than they expected. As I welcomed this man into our home I was trying to recall where I'd played a year and a half ago.

When the man sat down it was obvious that what he was about to say was difficult for him.

"I'm an alcoholic," he began. "It's been five hundred days since my last drink."

I didn't say anything. I didn't know *what* to say or why he was telling me this. And so I didn't say anything. I sat and I listened. He told me how he'd lost everything—his house, his family, his job, his car. He told me he'd sunk to scavenging the streets, picking up empty cans to get enough money to drink.

He said he'd gone to an Alcoholics Anonymous meeting

and tried to quit drinking. But after a few days, he said, he'd given up.

"I couldn't do it," he said.

Instead, he got a six-pack of beer and half a bottle of vodka and went into the bush. He told me he was already drunk when he got there and started in on the vodka and the beer. And, he said, that's when he decided to end his life.

"I put a gun into my mouth," he told me. "I had my finger on the trigger. I can remember thinking, I'm coming now, God."

He started to pull the trigger when he heard bagpipes. The pipes were playing "Amazing Grace."

"I stopped what I was doing," the man told me, "and I followed the sound of the bagpipes. They led me to your backyard."

It's rare, as you can imagine, that people drop in to listen to me play the pipes. My wife says she does remember someone briefly showing up one day around that time.

The man told me that after he left our backyard he went back to AA and someone, his sponsor I think, told him to write down everything he could remember about that Friday evening. He told me that this time he'd stuck with the program and that visiting me was part of his milestones to recovery.

I never met him again. He's moved out of town. But I think of him often and hope he's managed to stay away from alcohol.

Angus Campbell
Fort McMurray, Alberta

LOST IN TRANSLATION

Many moons ago, when I was a young university student, I spent a summer working in Berlin. This was well before the Berlin Wall came down, back when armed guards in watchtowers were on the lookout for refugees trying to flee to the West. At that time, West Berlin was home to a large number of Turkish workers who'd been granted work permits during periods of labour shortages. This is how I met my friend Ahmed.

Ahmed and I worked side by side in a paper factory. We worked on the packaging line. As we got to know each other, Ahmed expressed a wish to learn English. Well, I wanted to learn Turkish. So we began tutoring each other using our somewhat limited grasp of our only common language—German.

The best time for us to practise was during mealtimes. Whenever our shift broke for lunch we would sit together and talk. We talked about our homes, our families, and our dreams. Ahmed was just as curious about the Great White North as I was about his intriguing and mystical homeland.

Most days at lunch the workers would pass around a little of whatever they'd brought to eat that day. It created a mini-smorgasbord. It was during my second or third week that Ahmed pulled out a container of what looked like tinned tuna gone horribly wrong. Since Ahmed's proficiency in English was about as well-developed as my Turkish, it took considerable coaxing and a lot of bizarre hand gestures before I finally agreed to try a small piece.

I just about fell off my bench. After a spartan student diet (which back in Canada consisted primarily of beer, Kraft Dinner, and beer), my first taste of halvah was the most sensual food experience I'd had in months.

Over the course of that summer, Ahmed brought in an increasingly delicious parade of halvah that his wife would prepare for him. I would savour every piece as I attempted to make good on my promise to teach him my mother tongue. After a while, I had the idea that I should read to him.

The only English book we had was one that Ahmed had bought at a flea market: a battered copy of John Cleland's *Fanny Hill,* a ribald and explicit memoir of a young woman's introduction to sex and romance in eighteenth-century London. The bookseller had apparently handed it to Ahmed with a nudge and a sly wink, but as far as I figured, Ahmed had bought it thinking it was a run-of-the-mill novel that would—given enough time—allow him to master the intricacies of English. Ahmed was of a religious faith that tends not to discuss racy matters in open company. I felt compelled to choose my words carefully so that I wouldn't offend him. Whenever I came to a particularly graphic episode, I would incorrectly translate the passage as a detailed description of the room's furnishings ... scrupulously avoiding any mention of the acrobatic activities taking place therein.

Ahmed would methodically chew on his wife's halvah and listen carefully as I slowly read aloud to him, his eyebrows furrowed in concentration and his rough-skinned fingers slowly combing his thick black beard. It was during these long and rambling passages that I would sometimes see him glancing at me out of the corner of his eye with a puzzled expression. Perhaps he was wondering just what it was about mahogany table legs that was making an eighteen-year-old Canadian blush and squirm. One can only imagine what was going through his mind as I described the "group setting" in the living room.

My time in Berlin eventually drew to a close. As I punched out for the last time, Ahmed came over to say goodbye. He was holding two small packages in his burly arms. The first was a half-kilogram selection of his wife's finest halvah, given with her best wishes for a safe journey home. The other contained our English "textbook," for (as Ahmed put it) he hadn't found it to be anywhere near as interesting as the bookseller had promised. Besides, it seemed to him that I had enjoyed it considerably more than he had. Perhaps, he said— as he shook my hand emotionally in farewell—he would take up Italian instead.

Thomas Winterhoff
Victoria, British Columbia

STRIP SEARCH

In the summer of 1969, I was a camp counsellor.

We had a search protocol that we practised on a regular basis so that we'd be prepared in the event of a missing camper.

At the beginning of the summer, the staff was divided into two teams: "land search" and "water search." Each person had a specific area of the camp or waterfront to check. If you were conducting a water search, you had to duck-dive your way through the swimming area, all the while hoping it was just a drill.

Searches were signalled by an ear-splitting siren. When we heard the siren, staff members were expected to begin checking their assigned areas immediately.

Understandably, not everyone was dressed for a water search at all times. As a result, the usual practice was to peel off our clothing down to our underwear while sprinting for the water. Ours was a girls' camp and the staff was all female, so this didn't present a problem.

However, on one occasion, the siren sounded at the precise moment that canoeists from a boys' camp were blithely paddling by just outside the swimming area.

First, their ears were assaulted by the siren. After that got their attention, young women began running toward them, ripping off their clothes. The canoeists gaped at us, stunned, then oars flew in all directions as they tried to paddle the canoes closer. After being at a boys' camp for most of the summer, those boys must have thought they'd died and gone to heaven.

Once we got over our initial shock at having such an attentive audience, we plunged into the water and conducted our search. Fortunately, it was only a drill.

Judy Dryden
Victoria, British Columbia

MY MOTHER,
THE PILOT

I grew up in Charlottetown in the sixties, and until recently it never occurred to me that my mother wanted to be anything other than what she was. Now, however, it's obvious that her secret aspiration was to become a pilot.

My mother knew how to have a good time. During hot summer days she would take us to the beach. She'd pack a lunch, my four sisters and I would round up as many of the neighbourhood kids as we could fit into the car, and we'd be off. First we dropped my dad (usually in the front seat with two or three kids on his lap) at the office. The look of relief on his face as he slid out of the car and waved goodbye was never obvious to me then either.

On the way home from the beach we'd count Holstein cows—isn't that what everyone does on a car ride? But the sheer joy didn't begin until we came closer to town and my mother took us on a shortcut through what was, and still is, called "the Experimental Farm"—a test site owned by Agriculture Canada. We stopped by the building where they kept the "hens with glasses on" and we clambered out of the car to sneak a peek. Seven or eight sunburned kids and a tall freckled woman in a two-piece bathing suit crept up a little incline to peer in the dusty windows of a circular building. "I see them!" one of my sisters yelled, and we all scurried over. It was dark in there. I don't truthfully remember seeing any of the hens wearing glasses, but I know they were there. My mother said so.

When we got back in the car, the excitement mounted. I insisted on sitting next to a door. We all knew what came next. This particular portion of the road through the Experimental Farm had a lovely little downhill slope. Just the right distance to gather a bit of speed. Near the bottom was a railway crossing, with a rise up to and then down from the track.

My mother would choose a co-pilot from one of the squirming sticking-to-the-vinyl-seat-in-a-bathing-suit kids, and then holler things like "Pilot to co-pilot, over!" Those of us in the back would clutch each other, especially the lucky ones who got to operate the wings, I mean the doors. Mom warned us about turbulence and then she began the countdown. "Five, four, three ..." My mother's foot hit the accelerator like you wouldn't believe. "Two. Lift off!"

Four doors flew open simultaneously. We'd lean toward the middle of the car, the wind rushing in and filling our ears. We were flying! Kids hollered and whooped. Sand flew everywhere. The Kool-Aid jug rolled on its side.

My sister Roslyn started to wail. Sometimes, for added effect and excitement, my mother would lean on the horn.

I always kept my head down. My sisters tell me that the wheels of my mother's car never really left the ground. Maybe.

All I know is that for a nine-year-old kid in the backseat, we *were* flying, really flying, and my mother was the pilot.

Sandra Schwartz
Dartmouth, Nova Scotia

THE MYSTERIES OF MERINGUE

A dear friend of mine once produced an oil painting of my mom's lemon meringue pie. The painting is titled *Jean Odlum's Lemon Meringue Pie*. It's fitting that Mom's pie has been immortalized this way, because her pie is the stuff of legend.

Let me explain.

My mom made hundreds of pies in her lifetime—many of the lemon meringue variety. But there were two that stood out so vividly in the memory as to inspire artistic interpretation. The first sparked the legend; fifty years later, the second founded a religion.

The first inspirational pie was baked back in the 1940s. Mom's was not a classic forties kitchen. She and my father lived at Triple Island, a lighthouse north of Haida Gwaii.

Mom was a seventeen-year-old bride when she stepped onto that rock, and she surely didn't know what she was getting into. But those were the best years of her life, up there with my dad, learning how to run a household that got grocery delivery once a month (if they were lucky) and how to delight in the simple things.

One of those simple things was the occasional pie, and of course, the one-of-a-kind, myth-making lemon confection that went down in our family history.

That soft-peaked masterpiece tasted so delicious that it over-shadowed all her pies, lemon meringue or otherwise. The filling danced on the tongue with such exquisite tartness that even a half-century later the thought of it causes puckering.

It happened well before my time, but I heard the story often enough to know there would never be another pie as mouth-scrunchingly delicious as that one. All my life, whenever an occasion warranted a lemon meringue pie, the subject of that particular pie (and of the impossibility of dupli-cating it) came up.

Mom's second lemon meringue miracle was baked in the 1990s. It was baked for friends visiting from Japan. We were all seated around the table while Mom stood and made the first cut.

As she drew the knife back and began a delicate sawing motion, the pie squeaked. She paused. With each movement of the knife, it squeaked. It squeaked on a slightly different note during the forward sawing motion than it did during the backward sawing motion. Everyone began to laugh. The more it squeaked, the more we laughed.

She slowed the knife down, but the squeaks only became longer. She sped the knife up, and the squeaks sped up too. The laughing continued, and Mom had to pause to catch her breath. Even our conservative Japanese guests were in tears by the time the final piece was cut. Later, we discussed our theories—I maintained that it was the flaky crust, while others were convinced that it was the meringue. We'll never know; the results can't be duplicated.

It was her first and only musical lemon meringue pie. And the subject of that pie, along with the Triple Island pie, always comes up whenever I attempt to make a lemon meringue. Mine are neither remarkable nor musical. They don't make you pucker. They don't make the slightest squeak. But they're important, because they inspire retellings of our family's pie legend.

And that means my mom, and her pies, can live forever.

Ruth Raymond

North Vancouver, British Columbia

SKATING WITH SINGH

Sometimes I think about a solitary man who lived in our town when I was a kid—a Sikh man who everyone called Singh. This was back in the late sixties, when my hometown, Amherstburg, was no more than a bedroom community tucked in the bottom corner of Ontario and linked to the rest of the country by a long, boring stretch of the 401 highway.

Singh was an exotic being back then—an enigma separated from the rest of the community by his appearance. He lived in an apartment that had been converted from a business; his living room was the windowed storefront. We kids knew this because we'd steal glimpses of him through a gap in his curtain as we walked by. I remember him sitting in a straight-backed chair next to a table on which sat nothing but a black telephone. I don't remember a television or anything else. In my memory he's just sitting there, alone, in the sparse room. And we, in our nine-year-old wisdom, would avidly discuss him and his turban, and the rumours about the length of his hair underneath it. I don't know where he worked, and I don't recall seeing him with any friends. I don't know if he had a car.

As was typical of most small towns in Canada, the arena was the main hub of community activity. The winter I was nine, Singh took up ice skating. It was with curiosity and cruel bemusement that we kids observed him during Sunday-afternoon and Wednesday-evening public skating—either in the roped-off beginners' area or hugging the boards on his way around the ice. Singh was always smiling, as if being so out of place—winter coat and mittens over his exotic cotton clothing—amused him, too. His progress was excruciatingly slow, and I'd wonder, as I glided past, what kind of pleasure he could possibly get from his sluggish, jerky trips around the rink; he was such an easy target for the mean boys. But Singh continued to show up at the public skating sessions, and eventually he got better—eventually good enough that he didn't have to hold on to the boards. He became a fixture that winter, and our interest eventually waned.

Today I remember Singh through the eyes of an adult—not as an exotic émigré, but as a man. I can't remember when Singh stopped showing up at the arena, or when he left town. And I wish I could tell him that I remember him. That I know now that with every wobbly slip of his blades on the ice he was reaching out to his community. I wonder about the night he might have sat in that straight-backed chair and decided to buy a pair of skates and go skating. I wish I could tell him that his unabashed vulnerability is now, to me, a symbol of generosity and kinship. And that I wonder if he still skates.

Jennifer Morrison
Burlington, Ontario

YEAR FOUR

THE SHIP PUB

It's early October. I'm waiting outside the Tax on Wheels office at the corner of Patrick Street and Hamilton Avenue in St. John's. I'm waiting for a musician from Quebec who I met a few days ago up at the top of Lime Street. We were standing side by side, staring down at a rainbow that was growing right out of the harbour.

I'm new to St. John's; I moved here a few weeks ago to study. I recognized the woman on the street from one of my folklore classes, and so I started up a conversation. She's also new to the city, and when she suggested going to the Ship Pub for folk music night I agreed without hesitation. So far my social exchanges have been limited to small talk at the corner store and front-porch exchanges with my neighbour.

It wasn't quite the social life I'd envisioned before leaving Toronto just four weeks ago. I'd imagined myself laughing over bottles of Blackhorse with my new friends at a dingy but quaint local bar—with Great Big Sea playing faintly in the background.

Instead, I've spent the past few weekends alone, driving up and down the coast—my station wagon keeping me company. The scenery is beautiful, but life is getting lonely. The Québécois musician could have asked me to join her on a tour of the local slaughterhouse and I would have accepted. I'm lucky that she suggested folk night at the Ship.

Folk night is a series that runs every Wednesday and is hosted by the St. John's Folk Arts Council. Each week a local musician headlines. Audience members are encouraged to participate during the open mic interludes. This Wednesday two brothers from Bell Island are singing traditional ballads.

The entrance is tucked into a staircase off Duckworth Street. Inside, there's an elbow-shaped bar, a small stage, and about ten tables filled with people quietly listening to the Bell Island brothers sing their ballads. The walls are painted dark red. They're covered with gold records—each one carries the name of a band that's played there. Bands like the Saddle Horses, Slow Coaster, and Lady Luck.

We choose a table at the very back of the bar and join another folklore student—an Irish cheese scholar from Beaver, Pennsylvania. Halfway through the second ballad a fourth student from the department joins our table. She's a Scottish step-dancer from Edinburgh, and she's doing her Ph.D. research on haggis. Her dancing shoes are in a beat-up plastic bag that she hangs from the arm of her chair.

The balladeering brothers wrap up early so that they can catch the last ferry back to Bell Island. When the clapping dies down and the stage is cleared, a woman from the audience takes the microphone. She's from Ferryland, and she runs a small café there. She sings a sad and beautiful Irish ballad that she learned from her father. The crowd roars with appreciation, but she only sings once.

I buy another round of Blackhorse beer for our table and meet a small, white-haired Irishman at the bar. We talk about Dublin, where I lived one summer, and then he insists on paying for my drinks. I protest, but he prevails, and he helps me carry the bottles to my table. The singer from Ferryland laughs and winks at me. I introduce the man to the other girls and soon our two tables have joined.

The stage is empty and the front door swings shut. With some encouragement the woman from Ferryland agrees to sing another ballad. She doesn't use the microphone and she doesn't stand onstage, she just sits on a bar stool, closes her eyes, and starts to sing.

The haggis scholar changes her shoes and gives us a dance. The white-haired Irishman sings a song, and the Irish cheese scholar from Beaver, Pennsylvania, accompanies him.

Then the musician from Quebec sings "Down to the River" and everyone joins in—well, almost everyone.

"What about Toronto?" the man next to me asks. "What does Toronto have to sing?"

Toronto, as it turns out, doesn't have anything to sing. I hadn't learned any ballads at the Parkdale bars and Queen Street watering holes of my recent past, and the last song I sang was either "Happy Birthday" or the national anthem.

Now the circle of strangers, from Ireland, Scotland, Canada, and the U.S., turn to me expectantly. I shrug my shoulders.

"I don't sing," I tell them.

They assume that I'm being modest and so they encourage me again.

So I tell them again, "I don't sing."

The man next to me asks, "What do you do then?" The

group listens and waits. I want to tell them that I know several magic tricks, or that I play the oboe, or that I'm more sports inclined—which is the furthest from the truth. Instead, I say quietly, "Well, I write?"

It comes out more like a question than a statement, but it's all they need. The group relaxes, the step-dancer starts step-dancing again, the Irishman leans back on his stool and sings another ballad, and the man next to me says, "There wouldn't be any songs, you know, if there wasn't anyone to write them." After that, he welcomes me to Newfoundland.

The four of us stay out late that night and then we do it all over again the next Wednesday, and the Wednesday after that, and eventually I start volunteering once a month on folk nights. I'm the one who takes your cover charge and hands out the raffle tickets. You won't see me playing the oboe or performing magic tricks onstage, but I'll be the first to greet you when you walk through the door.

Emily Urquhart

St. John's, Newfoundland and Labrador

AS TEARS GO BY

My dad has been a tree-planter all his life. He's never done anything else. The outdoors is where he was born to be. From March until October, it's just him and the mountains. In the winter, however, when the ground is too hard to dig and the terrain too treacherous to navigate, my dad is forced indoors. Lucky me.

Most weekends in the winter, I make the silent, hour-long drive "up island" with my dad to a cabin that he likes to rent on Shawnigan Lake.

Once we get to the cabin, we start a fire, make a pot of spaghetti, sprawl out on the L-shaped couch, and watch "the game" on the old fuzzy TV. During commercials, my dad picks up his old guitar and plays "Mr. Bojangles," "Time of Your Life," or some other song that he's taught himself. When I was little, I used to find this distracting. Now I've come to notice, almost enviously, how talented he is.

One weekend last February, when I was going through a particularly bad Rolling Stones obsession, I said during a commercial break, "Dad, do you know 'As Tears Go By'?" He pulled out a tattered music book and opened it to a page that he'd highlighted years ago. He showed me which frets to put my fingers on and waited patiently until I got the chords right—G, C, A7, D, C, E, D.

After practising quietly while my dad watched the end of the game, I took a look at the words and started singing softly while I strummed. The game now over, my dad turned his attention to me and said, "You're doing really well. I never knew you were such a good singer." I blushed and continued singing, louder and stronger than before. He joined in.

The compliment meant so much to me. My dad is confident and independent, and he has so much talent that it's sometimes intimidating. So to be able to do something that really impressed him, especially something that he knows a lot about, well, to me, that was a big accomplishment.

The last time I visited my dad—in the Vancouver Cancer Lodge where he now lives—he picked up his guitar and tried to play as he had last winter. But the drugs that have made his face swell and his body shrink have also made his hand shaky and unsure of the notes. Not long after he picked it up, he sighed sadly and put it back on its stand in the corner of the room.

Later that day I picked up the guitar and slowly tried out the chords that he'd taught me a year earlier. As my steady hand strummed the chords—G, C, A7, D, C, E, D—my dad watched me enviously.

Kala Vilches

Victoria, British Columbia

COCKLED!

When I was a boy growing up in England, my mother would often purchase cockles from the fish man. I loved them. When we moved to Canada, you could only get cockles in a jar with brine. They didn't taste anything like the fresh ones, but I bought them anyway.

Years later, I was working as a photographer at a university medical school. We had three photographers in the department: me, another senior photographer, and a rookie named Steve.

One day at work I went out and bought a bottle of cockles to have with my lunch. I was eating them with the other senior photographer when I looked at the cockles and remarked, "These look like something that's been cut out of a body." And that's when a light bulb went on.

I placed some of the cockles on a paper towel and headed for the morgue. I knew the man who ran it and I knew that he'd be up for a little fun. I asked him if he'd tell Steve that he'd just cut the cockles out of a body and that they had to be photographed right away.

Steve went into the copy room and turned on the light

box. The cockles sat there, waiting to be photographed. The man in charge played along, regaling Steve with stories of the growths.

After Steve took a few pictures I came into the room and asked what was going on. Steve told me that the cockles were rare growths.

I picked one up and remarked, "Wow! These look almost good enough to eat."

I popped one in my mouth.

It only took Steve a few seconds to realize he was the victim of an elaborate prank. We got along famously after that.

Rollie Haselden

Sidney, British Columbia

CANOE MEMORIES

My first memory is of being in a canoe.

I am no older than three. I'm on the bottom of a canvas-covered, wooden-ribbed cedar canoe, lying on an assortment of coats and life jackets. I awake to the sound of my parents' whispered voices, discussing the pickerel my dad had caught and brought into the canoe—the pickerel now tied to the stringer with the other fish, trailing along in the water.

I grew up in a large family with eight siblings and even more cousins, aunts, uncles, and grandparents. We lived in an isolated community comprising mostly Native people. Most of our activities centred on hunting, fishing, gathering berries, and cutting firewood.

As the youngest child, I was dragged along wherever and whenever my parents went fishing. From the time I was an infant until my teens, I would spend many hours in a canoe or a boat. It was on those trips that my parents would talk about our ancestors—tales of trips from James Bay to the interior of the Canadian Shield to the shores of Lake Superior. Stories of the Windigo, Manitou, and Nanaboozho, and why we had to put offerings out for these spirits that inhabited the land.

Those stories shaped my life, connecting me to nature and her beauty.

Today, with work and family competing for attention, I try to spend as much time as possible in a canoe, paddling remote northern rivers, exploring wilderness parks, and meeting other canoe enthusiasts from around the globe. The best trips are the ones with family and close friends, without pressure to cover great distances. These excursions into the wilderness bring back memories and clear images of my parents and the lessons they taught me.

Back in the canoe with my parents, I stayed quiet, maybe because I didn't want the enchantment of the moment broken. I felt safe and protected. The gentle rocking of the canoe, the swirling and gurgling sound of the paddle as it's pulled through the water, the fragrances of cedar and fish. As I watched Dad's strong, deeply tanned, callused hands clutch the paddle, propelling us forward, I was content to remain on the bottom of the canoe, pretending to sleep.

Glenn Nolan

Atikokan, Ontario

CANADIAN PORRIDGE

When I came to Canada, my older brother told me that Canadians were turned off by English people who went on about how good things were in England.

"You're in Canada now," he said. "Get used to the Canadian way of life."

My first job in Canada was at Bell Telephone. I was involved in a new twelve-hour-shift experiment. There was nothing wrong with the shifts themselves, but the way Bell organized it I was on nights one week and days the next.

So when I arrived at Fran's Restaurant that morning in 1973 for breakfast I was bleary-eyed and not with it. I had just come off a twelve-hour swing shift.

A sweet lady named Rose worked there as a waitress. She gave me a menu, and I saw "oatmeal porridge." I was concerned that this didn't sound much like English porridge, but I remembered what my brother told me and decided to eat whatever was served. I made myself promise not to compare it to English porridge.

Service was slow that day, and it seemed like an eternity before Rose shuffled over to my table with the bowl, unceremoniously putting it down in front of me with a small jug of milk. Hungry, I looked down at it, thinking that it looked more like molasses than porridge, but then I heard that little voice inside telling me that I was now in Canada and should do things the way Canadians do.

I ate the contents of the bowl. It seemed a bit sweet to me, and it was cold, but as I was about to complain, I heard that little voice again.

As I was sitting back thinking that life in Canada was going to take getting used to, Rose came over with a steaming hot bowl. She put it down, looked confused, and said, "What did you do with the brown sugar?"

Nigel Johnson
Toronto, Ontario

THE ART OF IRONING

Every Saturday night in the winter, my three older brothers and my dad used to watch *Hockey Night in Canada* while my mother did the ironing. That was when there were only six teams and the season ended before daylight started to stretch into the evening, giving us more time for chores.

I grew up on a dairy farm, and while hayfields, ponies, and apple orchards may have seemed idyllic for a child, life wasn't easy for a woman with four children. Especially for a woman who worked full-time at the hospital in town to ensure there was enough money to pay for university educations. Laundry had to be done on Saturdays. So early in the morning Mom worked at the wringer washing machine (I wasn't allowed to help in case my hand got stuck in the bars) and then hung the clothes on the line outside the kitchen porch. By late afternoon we were hauling in the frozen pieces and spreading the sheets, shirts, underwear, towels, and pants all over the house to thaw in time for the Saturday night ritual.

I didn't particularly enjoy hockey, and there really wasn't enough room for me anyway, since my dad sat in the one chair and my brothers took up the chesterfield. So I perched on a stool in the kitchen, watching my mother as she methodically ironed the sheets, the pillowcases, the jeans, and the shirts.

It was the shirts that fascinated me. She did all my dad's shirts—his one Sunday white shirt and his plaid work shirts, one for each day of the week. She religiously followed a pattern that I watched over and over again. Of course I wanted to iron too. My mother let me start with the pillowcases. They weren't all that interesting, but we had to make sure that I understood how to use a hot iron (one without steam) before we took the risk of scorching a shirt.

Eventually I made my way to the shirts. First was the collar—both sides. Then the panel on the back of the shirt at the top. Next the sleeves. Do the cuffs first—again both sides, then pick up the underseam, give the sleeve a good shake, and you'll find it lies nice and flat on the board. It's a bit tricky when you come to the part where the pattern narrows and you have to negotiate the tip of the iron around the little tucks. A well-ironed shirt will have a sharp line running from the shoulder to the wrist.

After pressing both faces of the button strips, fit the front around the end of the ironing board and you're almost done. Two fronts and then the broad, open back—long, smooth, easy strokes.

Of course, ironing like that came before polyester shirts— shirts that you can throw in the dryer, pull out hot, and quickly put on a hanger. Certainly, throughout my adult life I haven't been ironing shirts. It's not a talent one brags about to one's husband.

At least it hasn't been until the last few weeks. He's either walked out the door wrinkled, or occasionally pulled out the ironing board and struggled away—no technique, no understanding of the intricacies of the art of ironing. But his life has been so engaged and hectic recently that I decided to reveal my secret. He needs a freshly ironed shirt for every night that he plays the drums for Stuart McLean's *The Vinyl Cafe*. He doesn't have time to iron a shirt. He doesn't have time to do his laundry. He doesn't even have time to call his mother.

And so I find myself using the skills that my mother taught me so many decades ago. As I struggle with those pleats around the cuff, I begin to think as my mother must have thought. This is not just a man who lives in the same house, eats the same food, and takes turns walking the dog. He's the man I married. Each shirt becomes an intimate affair. I can smell his skin and recognize scents that only a wife can know.

My parents have both passed away. This holiday season my three brothers are getting together to watch a hockey game at the Air Canada Centre.

I was invited. I won't be going.

I'll be ironing.

Margaret Hamilton
Toronto, Ontario

AN ABSENCE
OF ERIKA

I met Erika at a little college south of Winnipeg. I was seventeen.
She was nineteen. We fell in love with a storybook sweetness
and intensity. We were together for less than a year before
she moved to Brandon, Manitoba. After a year of struggling to
keep up a long-distance relationship, we decided to let each
other go. We were no less in love than we'd ever been, but
our lives had begun to go in different directions. Our decision
seemed practical and it broke our hearts.

Erika became a nurse. I worked, studied, and travelled
before settling in Winnipeg. We had almost no contact for five
years, but I couldn't forget her. There weren't more than a
handful of days when I didn't think about her and wonder
where she was, how she was doing, and whether or not I
would see her again.

In the fall of 1999 I was broke, lonely, and depressed. My
parents invited me back to Youngstown, Alberta, to help them
with the harvest. I needed to get away from the city, so I drove
home to our farm and got straight to work. Mom and Dad
wanted to sell the farm, so I was glad to be there for what might

be the last harvest. Dad and I bailed hay, cultivated fields, fixed fences, and worked around the yard, but it was the harvest itself that I liked best. We started early and worked until after dark, and Mom kept everything going with the lunches and suppers she brought out to the fields. Dad thanked me every day for coming home to help. He said he couldn't have done it without me. (It turned out to be the best harvest my dad had ever seen. The following summer they sold the farm and moved to a little acreage near Linden, Alberta.)

Farming was good for my soul, and being home with my parents was just what I needed. The long hours on the tractor gave me plenty of time to think. I thought about Erika. I thought about where she was, how she was doing, and if I would see her again. I tried to come up with situations where we might meet up. But it was all make-believe, all in my head. I thought she might even be married by now. Once again I tried to let her go.

Two days later I stopped at the house to pick up my lunch and Mom met me at the door. "Guess who called?" she said, putting her arm around my shoulder. "Erika. She wanted your number. She said she was going to be in Winnipeg and wanted to meet you for supper. I told her you were here and that you'd call when you had the chance."

I called that night. We talked for more than two hours. I called her again a couple of days later, after the harvest was over. I stopped through Brandon on my way to Winnipeg and we had supper. We talked until it was late, trying to catch up on the last five years. I felt the goodness of it right down to my bones.

Months later Erika told me that she'd called me out of the blue because she was tired of wondering where I was, and how

I was doing, and if I still loved her. She didn't know if I was even in the country or whether or not I was married, but after five years of longing she'd had enough. She called me because she wanted to marry me.

One year later, she did.

Kurt Armstrong

Vancouver, British Columbia

SCOTCH ROSE

My father, Alfred Watson, came to Canada in 1911 from Northumberland, England. My mother, Morag Urquhart, grew up on the Isle of Skye in northern Scotland. She came to Kimberley, British Columbia, to visit her sister Margaret. Margaret was married to my dad's best friend. Mom didn't get back to Scotland for forty years. She married my dad and raised a large family.

In 1954 the family moved to Kaslo, on the shores of Kootenay Lake.

Mom and Dad were Christians. They both knew scripture from memory. Their Bible was well loved, with many passages underlined in red. Church and music were a big part of our lives.

They were also avid gardeners. Each spring the back fence was covered in bright yellow forsythia, deep purple lilacs, and cream mock orange. In May the cherry, apple, plum, pear, and apricot trees burst into delicate pink and white blossoms. And there were the roses! We had yellow ones, white ones, pink ones, red ones; we had climbing roses, bush roses, tea roses, and hybrid roses.

The air at our house was always filled with sweet perfume and the sounds of songbirds making nests. Our backyard was a glorious profusion of colour and fragrance.

As well as flowers, our vegetable garden produced prodigious amounts of food. Fall was a busy time for the family. We helped Mom can the fruit and store the vegetables in the root cellar. Every year our fruits, vegetables, and flowers took top prizes in the Fall Fair. We were kids growing up in a small town, with plenty to eat, little supervision, and the lake and beach a short walk away. It was paradise.

This peaceful, happy, and secure childhood came to an abrupt end one day in September 1960. I was thirteen. Mom, Dad, a young friend, and I had gone across the lake in our boat for a picnic. As we returned later that afternoon, the lake became choppy and the temperature dropped. The boat's engine had been having trouble. Dad exhausted himself pulling the cord to start it. When we got to our beach and pulled the boat up onto the sand, Dad picked up the motor and promptly fell over backward—dead from a massive heart attack.

Dad was buried in the cemetery in Kaslo. Shortly afterward we moved away—first back to Kimberley, and then to Vancouver. We grew up and went our separate ways. Seldom did we return to Kaslo.

In 1981 Mom passed away from cancer. We buried her ashes at the foot of Dad's grave. A memorial plaque marked the spot. Although a caretaker mowed the grass around the plots, the grave itself soon looked barren and desolate. I was sorry we couldn't be there more often to tidy things up and bring flowers.

Many years passed without a visit to Kaslo. Then, in an interesting twist of fate, my husband's parents chose Kaslo for their retirement. It gave us a reason to revisit my old hometown. I delighted in showing my children our old house and yard, the school, the park, and the beaches.

When I took them to the cemetery to show them where their grandparents were laid to rest, I was astounded. There was a huge rose bush beside the grave. It was divided in the middle and its two branches cascaded down over each end of the grave. Nowhere else in the cemetery was there such a rose, or any other flowering bush. No one had planted it. It had simply appeared, provided by a loving God who knew we couldn't be here to tend the garden ourselves. It's the Scotch Rose, with masses of white blooms, a favourite of my parents.

I never worried again about taking care of that grave. If God was watching over it, that was good enough for me.

Sheila Watson

Sundre, Alberta

BECKY, FROM KANSAS

More than twenty years ago, the tourism branch of the British Columbia government had a campaign called "Good Show." British Columbian residents could be nominated for being good hosts and ambassadors to visitors to our province. Little nomination cards were put in strategic places around our communities. Winners of the award were sent a little gold pin with the inscription "Good Host."

That summer, as I stood in a bank lineup with my sister, I admired the pins. I told my sister that I thought the pins were cool, and that I'd like to wear one. I didn't think more about it after that.

Later that fall, I received a Good Host pin along with a personal letter from the government commending my "exemplary excellence in the hospitality industry." I also received a copy of the original nomination letter, sent in by one Becky McGovern from Wichita, Kansas.

Apparently, Becky was visiting family in Vancouver and lost her purse in Stanley Park. Not only did a lovely young woman (yours truly) contact Becky, but she hand-delivered it to the door where she was staying. Needless to say my sister had done some creative writing. I'd never found or returned a purse.

I enjoyed my sister's joke and thought that was the end of it, but that Christmas I received a card from the fictitious Becky. The year after that, I heard from Becky again. Every Christmas since then, Becky has sent me a Christmas card. She's developed an astounding personality, and is such a fixture in our family that my parents ask every year, "Have you heard from Becky yet?" Becky is now a middle-aged woman who became a born-again Christian a few years ago and then an ordained pastor in her church. She loves to sing, square dance, and even moved to Beverly Hills one year to pursue her love of acting. Two years ago she remarried a fellow with six other wives and moved to Montana. She always includes a bit of advice about life. She has never been able to recall my husband's correct name or how many children I have.

I know my sister loves writing that card and probably composes new stories in her head about Becky for weeks ahead of time. I've kept them all, including the original letter. And of course I still have the pin.

My sister and I no longer live in the same town, and in our busy lives we don't talk that often. But every Christmas I'm reminded of that day in the bank—me dreaming of a silly pin and her dreaming up ways to make me laugh. Decades later, I'm still laughing.

Nancy Gunn
Keremeos, British Columbia

FULL CIRCLE

For twenty-five years I worked at a pulp mill in Terrace Bay, Ontario, until the mill shut down. I moved on—to Fort McMurray, Alberta, the modern-day version of the gold rush. Like so many others, I went there for work.

This story, however, takes place over thirty years ago—when I found myself in a hotel in Pickle Crow in Northern Ontario. I was just out of high school, and had my first job: I was the junior member of my survey crew. We would work all day, head to the hotel for supper, and then to the saloon for a couple of beers.

Even back then, I loved music. I had a cassette player and a clutch of my most listened-to tapes. Word got around that I "had music." I was invited to the bunkhouse where the work crews stayed. Back then there was very little TV, no radio, and no women to chase.

I entered the room. There was a haze of smoke hanging in the air. The whisky bottle was passed around. I've never smoked, and I wouldn't develop a taste for whisky until many years later. I sat there with my tape player in hand. I looked at these men. They could have been right out of a history book:

voyageurs, or those men who built the railway.

I was just a kid. Not a word was said. I put my prized copy of *Tommy* by The Who into the tape machine. The music played and we all sat back and listened, lost in our thoughts.

Tonight, here in Fort McMurray, many years later and many thousands of miles away, I lie in my comfortable bed in my wonderful hotel suite. I have my state-of-the-art wireless headphones on. I'm listening to a pristine, remixed, remastered CD of *Tommy*. The CD cover is signed "To Doug, from Pete Townshend." The music is wonderful. And my head is full of memories of that bunkhouse in Pickle Crow.

I'm a million miles away from my family and I'm listening to the music in my head. Nothing has changed. The moment and the memory make me happy. After a while I shut off the music and go for a walk. In these moments I'm saddened, as all of a sudden I realize that for better or worse, I've come full circle.

I try to rationalize these feelings. Eventually I become comfortable with the thought that, if you live long enough, life *continues* to go full circle. I'm just now able to grasp that concept. All is fine.

Doug Harper
Fort McMurray, Alberta

YEAR
FIVE

CHARLES THE GREAT

Some years ago, my husband and I finally fulfilled our dream of living on a farm. We were city people completely intimidated by the thought of raising livestock. So, we decided to start small with some hens and the requisite rooster. After all, we thought, how hard could it be to raise a few birds?

We were dreaming about brown, organic eggs the day we picked up our four-week-old chicks at the local co-op. They came in a cardboard box. It was obvious right from the start which one was the rooster. On the way home we were alarmed at the shrieks emanating from within.

We were relieved to find only minor injuries when we got home, but we were left with the unsettling feeling that we might be unleashing a poultry monster into our lives.

The henhouse my husband was building wasn't ready, so we put the chicks in a small pen in the basement, where they flourished. One day I went downstairs to find the little rooster running around the pen holding a dead mouse by the tail. It was almost the same size as he was.

We named our rooster Charlemagne. After a time he became Charlie.

When the henhouse was complete, the chickens moved in. As he matured, Charlie became very possessive of his girls. By the time the hens started laying those coveted eggs, we were terrified of him. To collect the eggs, I had to wait until the hens were out free-ranging and then take the back way out to the henhouse, sneaking from tree to tree. If Charlie spied me I'd have to make a run for it. He was ferocious. He was unrelenting. He would race to get in front of me, spread his wings, and then jump at me repeatedly, landing his spurs, more often than not, on my tender shins. Sometimes he would pretend he didn't notice me. He'd peck busily at the ground until I let my guard down and then he'd launch a rear attack. Eventually I armed myself with a water gun. A well-placed squirt in that beady eye would buy me some time.

Charlie and I carried on this relationship for some time, each winning and losing some, until the day he came down sick. I separated Charlie from his flock. He was too ill to protest. It saddened me to see my tormentor defeated. Over the next while I kept him under a heat lamp and put electrolytes in water, which I dribbled down his throat. He had no desire to eat, but I was able to tempt him with rice and peas that I cooked especially for him. Amazingly, Charlie recovered and was soon as mean as ever—although I think he softened a little toward me.

Charlie was eventually killed by a raccoon while defending his flock. He fought bravely. We didn't lose a single hen that night. We still live on the farm and we know a little more about raising chickens these days. There have been many other roosters and hens over the years, but there has never been another Charlie.

Susanne Robinson

Orillia, Ontario

THE MAN ON
THE HILL

My name is North de Pencier and I'm seventeen years old. I live on top of a big hill, between two rivers, so the only way to get anywhere is to walk down the hill. On my way down there's a house where people receive help and support. I don't know what common quality binds the people in this house; maybe they're recovering from illness or addiction, maybe they're being reintegrated into society after some traumatic experience.

The first time I walked down the hill, I noticed that there was an older man sitting outside on the porch. This man wasn't there every time I walked by, but I saw him at least three times every week. Whether it was winter or summer, he was always bundled up. He seemed to spend all his time people-watching. At first, I reacted the same way as everyone else who walked by. When the man said hello I ignored him. I've been indoctrinated with the "don't talk to strangers" mentality from a very young age, so I react with suspicion to any sort of contact from people on the street.

I began to wonder if the man recognized me. After all, he

saw many people come and go every day, and I was only one of them, just another teenager going down the hill. I wondered what he saw in the people he watched. He was the only point of stillness in a constant crawl of people.

I felt guilty about being so uncharitable. Finally, after about a year of passing him by, I began to answer his hellos. He would wave delightedly at me as I walked down the hill, and again when I walked back home again. I suppose it must have been exciting to get a reaction from one of the people who usually pretended he wasn't there. Soon, it was me who was saying hello as I walked by. He would blow me a kiss and wave, and no matter how cold or grey it was outside, I'd always be cheered that I'd met someone who cared about the people around him.

I went away this summer. When I came back my friend wasn't on the porch anymore. I looked for him all fall, to no avail. I considered writing to the residence where he lived to see if he was okay, but then I realized that I really had no right to approach a man with whom I'd never exchanged more than a hello and who lived in a house that was careful to maintain its privacy. Still, if the man on the porch of the house who always said hello is out there, I would love to let him know that I appreciated every wave, and that his presence on the way down the hill is missed.

North de Pencier

Ottawa, Ontario

GOOD CATCH

It was the night of my fourteenth birthday. I'd already had as much of a party as I'd been expecting. There was school the next day, and even though it was pretty early, I was tired. The only thing left to do was shower and go to bed. Modesty wasn't an issue at our house, and no one was around but my parents, who were watching TV, and my kid sister, who was already asleep, so I went upstairs to my room to undress. I wrapped a towel around my waist and held the two corners firmly on one side. I walked back downstairs, through the TV room to the stairs that led to the basement, where our home's only shower was.

While I was there, visitors came by to wish me a happy birthday. It was Mrs. Day and her fourteen-year-old daughter, Marilyn Day. Mrs. Day was Mom's best friend and my music teacher. She was, and still is, a darling woman. *Marilyn* Day was going to be my wife one day, though she hadn't realized that yet. For her birthday, just two months earlier, I'd given her one of those elegant, don't-play-with-it-it's-not-a-toy porcelain dolls. It was dressed in a white satiny dress with a bonnet. A wedding dress, I decided. It wasn't, but that didn't matter. The doll had dark, shoulder-length hair, just like Marilyn Day. The doll had deep brown eyes, just like Marilyn Day. The doll had a soft, demure expression, just like Marilyn Day. The doll *was* Marilyn Day, dressed for our wedding. It was as much of a hint as I could muster. She didn't get it, apparently.

The gift pleased Mrs. Day because it had prompted her daughter to clean her room so that the doll could be properly displayed, but for Marilyn, it was just another reason to bake something in reciprocation. Her mom brought her over on the night of my birthday to surprise me with a large box of homemade chocolate-chip cookies.

They sat down in the TV room with my parents to chat. Mom and Dad had apparently forgotten about me because they didn't let me know I had visitors. Not only that, they looked just as surprised as Marilyn and her mother did when I opened the door at the top of the stairs and stood in their presence wearing nothing but a wet towel held about me with one hand.

The room was suddenly silent. I noticed, with horror, Marilyn sitting in a chair facing me. In her lap was a brown cardboard box; on her face was the same stupefied expression as the rest of us.

I suppose Marilyn just didn't know what else to do to rid the room of this dumbfounded, choking sensation. At least her heart was in the right place when she stood and, with forced cheer, declared, "Hey, A.J.! I made you some cookies for your birthday. Catch!" She chucked the box at me.

I caught it—with both hands.

A.J. Mittendorf
Prince George, British Columbia

WE DANCED

When I first met Anita, four years ago, I was delighted to learn that, like me, she was interested in ballroom dancing.

We signed up for classes on Thursday nights at a local college. We quickly learned that we'd be acquiring two skills: the basics of ballroom dancing and the basics of communication.

Our instructors taught Anita and me several dances: the cha-cha, the rumba, the swing, the foxtrot, the waltz, and the tango. They stressed that if we wanted to succeed we'd need to practise on our own. So, we danced. Over many Saturday evenings we danced in Anita's kitchen and worked out the steps together. By "worked out" I mean we practised and fought over the steps as we struggled to get them right. There are few ways to get to know someone better than dancing. We discovered that Anita verbally counts out the steps to the dances and I intuitively feel my way through the beats. Many times I would wait, arms crossed, toe tapping, while Anita counted out the steps. This led to many disagreements.

Some of the disagreements we could resolve verbally, but others could only be resolved physically, as we danced.

One memorable February evening, after dance class, Anita was driving me home and we were verbally working out the steps for the chase turns in the cha-cha. We had reached an impasse and could only settle things physically. So Anita stopped the car and we stepped out onto the cold, icy Edmonton street. As we met in the centre of the road, our eyes locked and we squared off against each other. I took her hand in mine and placed my right hand midway down her back. She placed her left hand atop my shoulder and we danced, in our ski jackets, in the middle of the deserted street. The street-light was our spotlight and the frozen road our dance floor. Oblivious to the cold, we worked out the steps together in our different ways: Anita counted in her methodical manner, while I felt my way toward perfection.

I would never have imagined myself dancing on the frozen, forbidding winter streets of Edmonton. But I had found my partner, and we danced.

Mark Cross

Edmonton, Alberta

MY LIFE IN TRAINS

I grew up on a remote lake in northwestern Ontario. Our village was accessible only by rail or boat. When I was small, in the 1950s, we had two steam trains a day, one eastbound and one westbound. We could catch the eastbound just before breakfast, ride the hundred miles into Port Arthur, do our business and grocery shopping, jump on the evening train and be home that night. I was about six years old the year they took the steamers off the rails. I remember coming out past the Neebing yards and seeing the steam locomotives being busted up for scrap. I cried my eyes out.

Over the years, as the highways were built, the train service diminished. By the 1970s we were one of the only places along the line between Winnipeg and Thunder Bay with no road in or out. We went from two trains a day to one: eastbound Tuesday, Thursday, and Saturday, westbound Monday, Wednesday, and Friday. Soon enough they took our real train away and replaced it with a railiner. You know the kind: two cars with a combined engine/baggage car up front and a coach behind. Not a real train, but it got us to town and home again. Often the only passengers we saw on the train were retired railway guys riding on their passes.

Usually when I rode the train, I'd ride in the baggage car. I'd sit with the mailbags and the stray pieces of local express freight, chatting with Bernie, the baggage man. On one memorable trip, the engineer was eating his lunch out of a classic gunmetal tin lunchbox. As he was chewing the last of his sandwich, he turned to me and asked, "Ya wanna drive?"

Like any self-respecting fifteen-year-old, I said, "Sure!"

I sat down on the seat, my foot on the deadman's pedal. "Just keep 'er out of the ditch," he said with a chuckle.

I was fifteen years old and I was driving the CN train. It's a very strange perspective to see the rails disappear under you from the front of a railiner.

The engineer, having finished his sandwich, started in on a butter tart wrapped in waxed paper.

"Pull the whistle," he said. "There's a crossing coming up."

One short and one long pull on the cord. The whistle sounded just like what I'd heard all my life.

The butter tart now gone, the driver pulled out a package of Players Navy Cut and a set of Vaughn papers. He rolled himself a smoke. We all smoked hand-rolled in those days. Tailor-mades were a treat from town. The engineer seemed reasonably sure that his train was in good hands, so he reached into the pocket of his jacket that was slung over the back of the seat. Out of the pocket came a mickey of Hudson's Bay rye. Without a second thought, he twisted the cork plug. It made an *eek-eek* sound as he pulled it out. He took a long pull from the bottle. After wiping his lips with his sleeve and gasping gently, he reached out his hand and said, "You wanna slug?"

It was becoming clear why the train seldom, if ever, ran on time.

In a few years CN took the train off completely. The community that existed died along with it. We remained isolated until a logging road touched our lakeshore in the mid-1980s.

I still miss the train.

Tony Ickes

Atikokan, Ontario

THE TRUTH OF TOWERS

It was the summer of 1963. My father was in the Canadian Army, and we'd been posted to the little town of Soest, Germany. There wasn't much to do if you were a girl living on the Canadian Forces Base in Soest. TV was all in German, so nobody bothered getting one. We didn't even have telephones. There was a big Quonset hut that had been converted into a clubhouse called "the Teen Hut." It was a place where teens could hang out, dance, and play ping-pong or cards. But you had to be thirteen to belong to it. I was twelve. I longed for the day when I could walk through that door, select a Beach Boys tune, and show everyone that I could dance as well as my big sister, Hazel.

The day I'm writing about had nothing to do with the Teen Hut, but everything to do with showing Hazel that I was as grownup as she. The plan that day was to pack some sandwiches and go to the pool.

Of course, as soon as we got there Hazel and her friends ditched me and headed to the tower in the deep end. I watched in awe and envy as they climbed the big tower and plunged into the pool. I was paddling around in the "kiddie" end, bored.

I knew what I had to do.

I climbed out of the pool and headed to the tower. I got five steps up the ladder when I felt a hand on my shoulder. It was one of the lifeguards. BUSTED! He spoke English. He was stern with me. He shouted, "You cannot go up the tower! You are too small!" I argued with him. While I wasn't the strongest swimmer at the time, I knew I was capable of jumping from the tower and swimming to the ladder at the side of the pool. Finally he said, "Okay, you prove to me you can swim ten lengths of this pool and I will allow it!"

He blew his whistle and cleared a swath for me along the side so that I could start my swim. Now, this pool wasn't just an ordinary pool, it was an Olympic-sized pool. I climbed into the shallow end and started my Olympian feat. By the time I got to the end of my first length I was exhausted, but I was buoyed by the laughter and splashing made by the older kids—and Hazel—as they continued to jump off the tower. I managed to make it back to the other end of the pool without stopping. I desperately wanted to pause for a minute and take a breather, but I knew that if I did it would be the end of my tower dream. With great difficulty, I started out on my third length. My lungs felt like they were going to explode. My arms felt like they were detached from my body and working entirely on their own. My legs were the only part of me that worked as commanded. I tried to keep thinking about the tower and how much fun it would be.

And then it happened. I could feel myself beginning to sink. I remember thinking that if I could just keep my legs going

I'd be okay. By some small miracle, I reached the end of my third lap.

That's when I heard the whistle. It was the lifeguard. He was standing over me at the end of the pool. Pretending not to hear, I turned around, put my feet on the wall, and drove off mightily. I felt a hand on my bathing suit as he tried from the edge to pull me out of the pool.

I turned around and punched his hand away.

That gave me enough of an adrenalin surge to keep going. I could feel my arms again, and my lungs responded as well. I veered away from the edge of the pool, out of the lifeguard's reach, and kept going, knowing that this might kill me but I was darned if I wasn't going down without a fight.

And what a fight it was: two big lifeguards jumped in and dragged me out, kicking and screaming. They were yelling at me in German and wagging their fingers at me.

I responded by turning around and jumping back into the pool to resume my fourth length. They were waiting for me in the shallow end. This time I didn't have a chance. They forced me out of the pool, put a towel around me, and suddenly, good-naturedly, one of them said, "You have guts! I like you. You can jump off the tower. But take a rest first and be very careful!"

Twenty minutes later I was ready. Still wobbly from my ordeal, I approached the tower nervously. I knew I was being watched. I looked up. Funny, the tower hadn't seemed that big before. I put my foot on the first rung and began my ascent of the seemingly endless ladder. By the time I got to the top I could feel the adrenalin again. Finally, my dream had come true. I was "one of them"—a teenager! All the way up I rehearsed the perfect cannonball in my mind. And then, there

I was, on the platform. I walked over to the edge and looked down, ready to execute my plunge to glory!

I should *never* have looked down.

But I did.

I looked down, and then I turned around, climbed humbly back down the ladder, and strolled nonchalantly back to the shallow end. On the way, I felt a hand on my head. One of the lifeguards gave me a friendly hair rub. I turned around. He didn't laugh or make fun of me. He winked and smiled. I smiled back, feeling very grownup indeed.

Heather Henderson

Belleville, Ontario

CHOCOLATE
SPRINKLES

I grew up in Edmonton. I remember the houses on our street—
some were brown stucco bungalows with charming entrances;
some had sunrooms in the front with small, square panes of
glass looking out to the yard; some were three storeys tall with
mysterious-looking attics. Ours was a wartime house—one of
many built for the veterans who'd just returned from World
War II. It was a simple, solid, white clapboard house with
bedrooms upstairs and a front lawn that led to a boulevard
lined with protective elm trees.

It was 1954.

Although I didn't know the world had just changed, I could
see that our street was changing. There was a surge of new
people moving into basement suites, upstairs apartments, and
spare rooms. Families were arriving from the Netherlands. For
us it was wonderful, because there were so many new children
to play with. In those days, when I was about five, it seemed as
if children played all day long—mostly outside.

The Dutch kids didn't speak English, so our introduction
was a graceful dance of smiling, nodding, and curiously staring

at our different sweaters and shoes. There was a girl named Heddy who was my age. Heddy laughed hysterically when my brother made silly faces. She ran to get her sisters, and then motioned to my brother to do it again. He was pleased to have his silliness so happily received.

Before long we were showing them our best climbing tree, or where you could find discarded pop bottles that could be taken to the store and exchanged for candy.

They would point at things, then motion for us to say the English word. When we did, they would repeat it: *tree … grass … window*. We got them to say Dutch words that *we* could repeat, not one of which I can remember today.

My dad was a harsh man. His voice was loud. There was also a great sadness about him—a sadness that I didn't understand at the time. I remember telling him about our new friends. He said he'd been to Holland and told us we were to be good to those children.

Once I overheard my parents talking. My mom said, "You should see the garden—the fences are covered with peas and beans. Every inch of soil in the back is planted; potatoes to the very edge of the alley."

In a low voice, my dad said, "They know hunger."

One day, Heddy's mom said I could join them for lunch. I was delighted. We went to the back door of the house across the street, and as we stepped inside the melting aroma of freshly baked bread drifted up to meet us. The stairs creaked as we descended to their suite in the basement. Their home was two rooms—a tiny kitchen with white and yellow cupboards, a glistening linoleum floor, and crisp yellow curtains separating the kitchen from the bedroom. The small table was set with a sparkling white tablecloth. Everyone squeezed closer to make room for me. We all felt shy that day.

Heddy's family bowed their heads, and in their language, said a gentle, murmuring grace.

Her mom got up and brought food to the table. Warm, white, homemade bread, soft butter, sliced hard-boiled eggs, a plate of Edam cheese, and a bowl of chocolate sprinkles. I watched the others put together their sandwiches and I followed. I had never tasted homemade bread. I had never seen white cheese. I was astounded that people could be so brilliant as to think of adding chocolate sprinkles to a sandwich! I think they were surprised at the look of pure pleasure on my face. My sandwich was heavenly. And like the day my brother made them laugh, Heddy's family leaned back in their chairs and laughed out loud at how their lunch had pleased a little girl.

That winter, Heddy's family moved to a house in St. Albert.

For over forty years, on hot summer nights, my mom would sit on her front steps and watch the world go by. One night we sat together. She asked me if I remembered the Dutch families. I thought about how children reach out innocently, and can touch both the familiar and the strange, the old world and the new.

My mom remembered their garden. I remembered their chocolate sprinkles.

Wendy Everitt
Fort Saskatchewan, Alberta

LEARNING TO SKATE

I never learned how to skate. Growing up in southwest Saskatchewan, land of perpetual Chinooks, "good" ice didn't last long enough for me to get the hang of it. I'd try, tripping, falling, crawling to the edge of the rink to pull myself up. Some years I'd get the knack of forward, but I never figured out how to stop. I would crash into the boards when I needed a rest. So I grew up not knowing this most basic Canadian skill. It never bothered me, until now.

Now I'm a Canadian mother. And not just a Canadian mother, but a *northern* Canadian mother. And, while there are some things missing in a community that's over 350 kilometres from the nearest Tim Hortons, one thing we have plenty of is ice. Six or seven months a year. Acres and acres of lake ice and a big rink that's always filled with NHL hopefuls.

This year the town cleared the snow from two empty lots, one on either end of town, and flooded them, making two mini-rinks just for the little kids. No teenagers allowed. Plenty of opportunity to learn to skate.

One sunny Saturday afternoon in mid-January, my husband and I headed down to the rink with our two boys—aged ten and six. We sat on the snowbank and laced up their skates. We checked to make sure they had mitts and toques. The older one stepped out somewhat cautiously, but was soon on his way. The younger one … I don't know. I couldn't watch.

I peeked between my fingers as he took one or two faltering steps and crashed to the ice. He bounced back up as if he were on springs.

Another step or two and down again. His dad and I cheered from the banks every time he got back up. The scene repeated itself over and over until, by the end of half an hour, he was making it from one end of the rink to the other in his high-stepping, trotting way.

He cried when we told him it was time to go home, that his feet would be sore and his body would hurt if he kept going. He insisted that we take him back after supper so that he could practise some more. He's probably skated more in the last month than I have in my entire life.

And that's when I knew, watching him that night skating in the dark, that there are so many things my boys are going to need to learn that I won't have a clue how to teach them. I'll do my best to supply them with the tools and to introduce them to the folks who know the ropes. But then I'll just have to stand by and watch through my fingers as they fall, pray that they get back up again, and cheer when they do. I'll have to learn to not interfere when they're surrounded by those who are bigger, faster, and stronger. And let them go, even when every ounce of my being shouts at me to hold them close. I'll have to stand by the side of the rink, and watch them skate.

Cheryl Glass
Pinehouse Lake, Saskatchewan

CHRISTMAS PACKAGE

I listened to your story of Stephanie's trip to London yesterday on *The Vinyl Cafe*. I too was brought up in London after the war, and Dorothy's description of the Christmas parcel from Canada reduced me to tears.

You see, we also got Christmas parcels from a cousin in Canada. Forever known as "René's parcels," they arrived for four straight years in the middle of November. I remember the day the first one came in the mail. We'd been out for a walk, Mum and I.

That's what you did during the war: walked around all the shops to see if they had anything—food or fuel—to buy. When we got home, tired and cold, my grandmother said a parcel had come for us, from René.

The package was in the front room. Coal was rationed at the time, so we used to heat only one room. I remember opening the door of the front room and being enveloped in a rush of cold and a wonderful smell. When I asked Mum what the smell was she said it was from all the pine trees in Canada. For years, that's how I thought of Canada—cold and pine trees.

The parcel was carefully sewn into a flour sack, which Mum

painstakingly unpicked stitch by stitch while I danced with impatience.

I was about four at the time and had only heard about the wonderful Christmas presents wrapped in colourful paper that would come my way when the war was over. To me the parcel contained all the riches of Araby wrapped up in a flour sack.

Eventually Mum got the sack, covered in colourful stamps, unpicked. She set it carefully aside. She later made the sacks into tea towels, aprons, and pillowcases. But now she began to carefully open the cardboard box inside.

And instead of the riches of Araby wrapped in coloured paper there was—food! I was a bit disappointed at first. Until Mum began removing the contents. She and my grandmother exclaimed over every item. There was a Christmas cake laden with dried fruit, and a one-pound bag of sugar—more sugar than we'd had at one time since rationing started. The parcel always contained things that were rationed, in short supply, or just unobtainable—all things I'd never seen. And there was always one small present for me—a comic book, a leather bag, a pair of fancy hair barrettes that were so unusual people would stop Mum in the street to ask where she'd got them.

One year there was a chicken in a glass jar—a wonder indeed. As Mum took it out of the box she said, "Here's our Christmas dinner," and it was. Together with the Christmas pudding it made a festive meal.

Then there was the year Customs opened the box, the first and only time it happened. They included a note telling us they'd searched the parcel, but in the search they cut open the paper bag of sugar. They put it in another bag and put it back of course, but it had spilled all over the box and its contents. Mum spread a cloth on the table and wiped the sugar off each item. Then she carefully flattened the box and shook each grain of sugar into a bowl, going over each seam and fold again and again to make sure no grains were missed—all the while tears pouring down her face at the unfairness of it all.

Mum cried again at the end of the war when René wrote to say she'd heard that things were back to normal in the U.K. now that the war was over and she didn't think we needed any more parcels. I wanted Mum to write and tell René that conditions were still dreadful. Mum explained that the cost of the food and the postage were probably too expensive for René, so we wrote and thanked her for her help instead.

Eventually I visited René and her family. Later, I moved to Canada and met my husband. I've been here ever since.

When René passed away a few years ago, instead of placing flowers on her grave, I placed a small box wrapped in Christmas paper.

I got a few odd looks, but René, my mum, and I knew what it meant … and that's all that mattered to me.

Peggy Halstead
Winnipeg, Manitoba

DRIFTING HOME

This afternoon, at the stable where I keep my horse, some women were reminiscing about things they'd done back in their twenties. One recounted buying a farm with her husband and another couple. She went on at length about the hardships and dreariness of farming in the winter: the trials of deep snow, the tribulations of mucking out and feeding cattle.

I grew up on a dairy farm. As I drove home that night I began to reflect on the bleakness of dairy farming in mid-winter. The mornings always began in the darkness. Windows had to be left open because of the coal furnace, so I used to jump out of bed and run down and stand in front of the wood stove while Mom put my clothes on. Of course Dad had been out the door two hours earlier to do the milking. Frozen pipes, empty cisterns, wet woollen mittens, rubber boots with no linings, dinners of macaroni and cheese or potato soup—all were facts of existence, never questioned or thought about.

But then, of course, not all of winter was adversity. We could ride on the toboggan behind the work horses, not even noticing the manure. Or, when we did, just the warm fresh scent—all sweet and leathery. There were forts and tunnels in the snowbanks, and quick, hard snowballs thrown when Mom and Dad weren't watching.

Most special of all were the afternoons when we trekked down to Stainton's pond, built a fire, and skated, slapping pucks between the boots we set up as nets. I learned how to skate while Ken Stainton held me between his arms in hockey skates handed down from my brother (toes stuffed with newspaper so they'd fit). For those few hours the boys were Frank Mahovlich, Rocket Richard, the Pocket Rocket, Davey Keon, Gordie Howe, and Boom Boom Geoffrion.

While my brothers were dreaming their way to Maple Leaf Gardens, Mom frequently sent me to take a bag of apples to Mrs. Mabel Wright. Mrs. Wright was confined to a wheelchair, but she still had to bake her weekly pies. I didn't mind the walk north up the hill because it led me into the steamy warm kitchen of Mrs. Stainton. Lean, tough, and no doubt exhausted, she always greeted me with a delighted smile and an insistence that I come in and sit. It was one of those kitchens that seemed to go on forever. I would slip into a wooden chair and watch in wonder as she reached up to the shelf on the top of her Quaker stove and pulled down trays of hot cinnamon buns. Of course I had to have one, and I had to have it with butter. I often wished I could stay there, in that room wafting with rich and effusive aromas. She always took the time to wipe her hands on her apron and ask me how I was. She was concerned if I had a cold or had lost weight after suffering from the mumps.

She was what I imagined a grandmother might be, except that she wasn't old. As a child I could only think that she must be the perfect mother. Why did mine always have something for me to do—another chore? More piano?

Mildred Stainton, in my childhood mind, was forever in her kitchen, kneading dough, pulling magical culinary wonders out of her oven, and inviting me in.

Of course as an adult, I know that Mrs. Stainton was a mother too, and as a mother she would have made the same demands on her three sons that our mother made on us. Both struggled with the poverty of farm life and both tried to lead their children to easier lives. Their foundation of unrelenting support gave all of us confidence and an undeniable reassurance that we could become whatever we wanted. And, yes, my life is easier than my mother's. Yet as "dreary" as farm life may seem to some, without a doubt, what makes my life so satisfying as an adult are the memories of those winter mornings, the snow drifts, the pond, and the cinnamon buns.

Margaret Hamilton

Toronto, Ontario

AIR MAIL

YEAR
SIX

CLASS PICTURE

Every once in a while I like to dig out my old class pictures. I have a laugh at the hairdos, shake my head at how things have changed, and grow quiet as I let those long-ago images of elementary school take me back into the swirling, misty moments of time past.

Grade three. South School. I walked to South School every day, across the wooden footbridge over the trickling Waskasoo Creek, always a stick or branch in my hand, always pausing to spit into the little creek off the little bridge. Spitting off the footbridge was an essential, instinctive ritual that seemed to be restricted to the specific social group known as "boys on their way to school."

Often, I would walk with Glen. Glen lived in a broken-down house (more of a shack really) down the street from me. If the timing was right, we'd join up on our way to school, kicking rocks down the sidewalk in the fall, throwing the odd snowball in the winter, floating little matchstick boats down the gutter rivulets in the spring.

We never said much to each other. Glen wasn't much for words. He'd been "held back" a grade or two in school and was taller and bigger than the rest of the grade threes. To me, he always seemed a bit embarrassed about that, slouching in the little desk in Mrs. Lougheed's class.

But everyone liked Glen—and everyone liked his dog, Blackie. Blackie was a big old black Lab, as quiet and gentle as Glen himself. Outside of school, the two were never apart.

Often, Blackie would walk Glen and me to school, and then make his way back home by himself. Often Blackie would be there all by himself at the end of the school day, waiting to walk us home again. Those days with Blackie were Glen's favourite days. Mine too.

Blackie wasn't supposed to be at the school, though. Glen's mom had been told that dogs weren't allowed on the school grounds, and Blackie didn't have a licence or even a collar for that matter.

There'd been a couple of incidents with dogs biting kids at the school, but we all knew that Blackie would never bother anybody.

One spring day, the recess bell rang and I looked out the classroom window and saw Blackie sitting in the school-yard. He was sitting in the shade by the baseball diamond. He'd heard the bell too, and that big old tail started wagging because he knew Glen would soon be there.

When the bell rang we all ran out of the classroom to the yard.

Glen made a beeline straight for Blackie, with me right behind him. We were both instantly rewarded with a woof and a lick, but Glen was worried. He told Blackie to go home, that he wasn't supposed to be there, that he would get into trouble. Glen never raised his voice, he just told Blackie very serious-like. Blackie knew he was in trouble. But Blackie wasn't going anywhere.

By this time, most of our grade three class had gravitated over to Blackie, kneeling down for a hug, hoping for a lick on the cheek. The most popular girl in the class, Penny Bond, was on the receiving end of a mighty slurp when we heard the sound of wheels on gravel.

The van pulled up right beside us. It was the dogcatcher.

"I have to take the dog," said the dog catcher as he got out of the van.

He was carrying a pole with a loop of rope on it. It looked like a noose to me.

Nobody moved. Blackie woofed.

Glen kneeled beside Blackie, hugging him.

"He's my dog," said Glen. "It's okay. He's my dog, Blackie."

But the dog catcher took a step toward us, slowly swinging the pole. "I don't see a licence on this animal. He doesn't even have a collar. I have to take him to the pound, kid. If he's your dog, you can claim him there, pay the fee and claim him at the pound."

Glen was trying really hard now not to cry in front of all his friends. He didn't want to say that his mom didn't have the money to get Blackie out of the pound. He didn't want to say, If you take Blackie now, *nobody* will get him from the pound. He didn't want to say it, but we all knew what happened to dogs that nobody claimed from the pound.

The dog catcher wasn't listening. He took another step toward Blackie. Glen started to cry. Suddenly, somehow, we all stood in front of Glen and Blackie. We stood between them and the dog catcher. And then Penny Bond grabbed my hand,

and I grabbed someone else's hand, and we all linked together and formed a circle—a huge circle of grade three kids, arms outstretched, building a human fence around our friend and his dog.

It was one of those moments. One of those moments you know you'll always remember, even when you're old. Especially when you're old.

We stood there, Glen and Blackie in the middle of that circle, the dog catcher outside it, not exactly sure what to do. Nobody said a word.

We would have stood there forever if it wasn't for Mrs. Lougheed. Somehow she was out the back door of the school and calling to the dog catcher. They stood by his ugly orange dog catcher van, and although we couldn't hear what they were saying, we could see that they were having more than just your everyday, normal, boring adult-type conversation.

We hung on to our circle even harder. And then something amazing happened. The dog catcher got into his van and drove off. He didn't say anything to us at all; he didn't even look over at us. He just drove away.

When the cheering, and hugging, and crying died down, Mrs. Lougheed got us settled down in the classroom, Blackie sprawled in the corner at the back of the room, snoozing away contentedly for the rest of the afternoon. I'd never seen Glen so happy.

Blackie never went on the school grounds again. He would wait for Glen on the boulevard across the street, in the shade. Blackie was smart that way.

Glen and his dog and his mom moved away that summer, and I never saw them again. But every now and then, I take out my old cardboard box of memories and pull out my grade three class picture. If you look closely, there with all the silly smiles and goofy hairdos and proud and shiny eight-year-olds is an old black dog curled up at the feet of the biggest kid in the class.

Harley Hay
Red Deer, Alberta

JIGGIN' FOR SQUID

My first parish as an Anglican minister was in the small outport of Trinity East on the north shore of Trinity Bay, in Newfoundland and Labrador.

My wife, Karen, and I had just moved from Toronto, and I soon realized that we could fit all the residents of Trinity East into one Toronto subway car.

I lived there in the early nineties, a time when the folks in Ottawa were making decisions about the future of the fishery. I would sit at kitchen tables in the homes of my parishioners and listen to them talk about their future. I knew that in order to do this job well I had to learn about the fishery. And what better way to find out about the fishery, and those who make their living by dory, than to get out on the ocean and see for myself?

It was cold at dawn on the morning I went out. I stepped into the boat and waited for the three cups of coffee to take effect. One of my parishioners, Ray, started his Mercury outboard and off we went.

I felt excited about this adventure. We rode for an hour in the boat, and I wondered where we were going. Ray knew.

He was looking for the seagulls, which, he said, always knew where the squid were swimming.

Ray soon stopped the motor. He looked up at the gulls circling above.

"Put down the jigs," he said.

There were four large spools on gunwales, rolled with hundreds of metres of heavy fishing line. Every thirty centimetres or so there was a small hook, a jig, which would grab onto any part of the squid's body. It was crude but effective. I let down the line until I was told to stop.

My captain told me to rock the spools back and forth, back and forth, until I felt the weight of the squid on the end of the line.

"Haul her up!" Ray shouted.

I could not have been prepared for what I was about to see and hear. Squid, all about the size of my hand, came flying off the jigs into the bottom of the boat, their gills gasping for water.

There were more squid than I'd ever seen in my life.

I could tell by the look on Ray's face that this was a good catch. Ray looked happy. I was proud and honoured to be part of this day.

"Now what?" I asked.

"Well, my son," he said, "now you got to separate the males from the females."

"How do we do that?" I asked him.

"Well," he told me, "if you pick them up and look closely through their tentacles, just below their eyes, you can see the difference."

It sounded reasonable to me. I'd taken enough marine

biology as an undergrad to know that, yes, it was possible to tell the difference between a male and a female squid. As a minister, I knew that God had created them so.

What I'd forgotten, however, was the sophisticated defence mechanism that squid and other cephalopods had developed over millions of years of evolution. It was sophisticated, though not very precise.

But when you're a squid swimming through the cold waters of Trinity Bay, when you're a squid trapped in the bottom of a dory, gasping for air, when you're a squid being picked up by an Anglican minister who until very recently lived at Broadview and Gerrard in downtown Toronto—you don't have to be very precise. I picked up a squid and tried to determine its gender.

"You might have to hold it closer," Ray told me.

That was the last thing I remember hearing.

The ejection, if not precise, was certainly thorough.

It was thick, cold, and too salty to describe. It splashed over my face, covered my eyes, went further up my nose than I care to remember. It tasted like nothing I'd ever tasted before. The fact that it got into my ears surprised me.

With my ears clogged I could hear only one sound rising above the squishing sound of the squid on the bottom of the boat. It was my captain, my very much amused captain, laughing harder than he had for a long time. My initiation into the community had begun.

Michael Calderwood

Brighton, Ontario

OVER THE RAINBOW

Every time I hear "Over the Rainbow" it brings tears to my eyes, for a very good reason.

Nineteen eighty-one was a bad year. My husband died early that year and, a few months later, in July, I almost lost my eldest son, Nick.

Nick was a music student at Mohawk College in Hamilton.

He was born with a medical condition that we became aware of when he was seven. Because this condition limited him physically, he quickly fell in love with music. Music was Nick's life.

A few months after his father's death, Nick became ill and went into the hospital in Hamilton.

The neurosurgeon told me that Nick needed surgery, but that the risk was high and if he survived he could be completely or partially paralyzed.

Nick's brother and I sat through the six-and-a-half-hour surgery in the hospital waiting room.

Finally we were told that Nick had come through okay but that we'd have to wait and see regarding his mobility.

A day later Nick slid into a coma. He'd had a stroke. He

did recover, and was eventually sent to another hospital for physiotherapy, but the prognosis was bad. He was told that he most likely wouldn't walk again and that he'd never again play the piano.

Nick went into a deep depression. He refused to talk to his music teacher or students from Mohawk. He wouldn't even *listen* to music.

His brother and I tried to encourage him; we told him he had to believe in himself. We told him that anything was possible.

Months passed. Each Sunday I would leave my home in St. Catharines and go and visit Nick in the hospital.

By the time six months had passed, Nick was able to talk and "walk" himself around the hospital in a wheelchair.

One Sunday I arrived at the ward for our visit and found that Nick wasn't there. I was desperately worried about him until one of the other patients said he'd gone down to the common room.

I hurried down there and found Nick sitting at the piano. He was trying to play "Over the Rainbow." His fingers were collapsing on the keyboard and tears were streaming down his face. This was the turning point for him. After another six months of therapy, Nick came out of the hospital and returned to complete his degree at Mohawk College.

At the graduation concert Nick walked onto the stage, threw down his canes, limped to the piano, and played a concerto he'd written. He received a standing ovation. It was the proudest day of my life.

Brenda Baltensperger
Calgary, Alberta

A TINY SILVER BIRDCAGE

I grew up in Berlin, East Germany. My parents, both stage designers by profession, spent most of my childhood talking about leaving East Germany for West Germany.

This was a crucial decision, because there was no way back. Once you left East Germany you couldn't return home. We were subject to the most severe travel restrictions. We weren't allowed to travel to Western countries, which made it nearly impossible for people to cross the border.

I witnessed my parents wrestling with this. Numerous times they claimed that they'd made the final decision to stay or to go. And then I would watch them change their minds for various reasons. Even as a child I was able to tell that this wasn't easy for them.

I wasn't convinced that the predicted paradise truly existed on the other side of the wall. But I began to replace my parents' escape fantasy with one of my own. I too began to focus on something in the West, but way farther west than my mother and father were aiming. The first word I wrote, at the age of five, wasn't my name. It was "Canada."

My East German kindergarten teachers were not amused with my growing admiration for a land that was considered part of the evil West. They confronted my parents and asked them why their son was writing "Canada" everywhere he could: in the sand, on the wall, on the table, even on the skin of my palm. My parents couldn't explain it; they had no clue where it came from. They suspected that my aunt, who worked at the public library, may have given me a book with the alluring maple leaf on the cover.

At school I was more familiar with the shape of the St. Lawrence River and Hudson Bay than with the geography of my own country. I begged my mother to stitch maple leaves onto my clothes.

My parents were still thinking about how to escape our socialist country. In early 1989 they made their most serious attempt. They used a fake invitation to an exhibition in West Berlin to apply for an artist visa. As soon as they received the permit to cross the border, they packed the car with exhibits. The documents they would need for the new start in West Germany—like birth certificates and proof of their degrees— were hidden underneath the costumes of the fairy tale marionettes. The plan was that my father would "officially" escape, meaning he would announce to East German officials his desire to stay in the West after he became a registered refugee there. Afterward, the rest of the family would apply for permission to follow him.

This was one of the known procedures East German people used to leave the country illegally.

My father ended up in a refugee camp in West Berlin. He was anything but happy. He had to live with four other men in a narrow shipping container. He missed his family and his house.

He'd never been convinced that leaving the East would be the best idea. The situation he found himself in made him feel even more doubtful. When he implied this in several phone calls with my mother and then told her that he was close to returning, she decided to mount an attempt to rescue the plan.

If the guards would let her cross the border with her own visa, she would visit my father, cheer him up, and convince him to stay. With this intention she left my sister and me for a day trip to the western side of the Berlin Wall.

She achieved the opposite of what she'd hoped; my father's yearning to be reunited with the family grew even stronger when he saw his wife. It began to dawn on my mother that the plan was failing.

She made two more trips to see my father. After the third visit she realized it would most likely be her last.

She walked through the streets of West Berlin in despair. East German officials would never allow them to travel again after this illegal escape attempt. In her resigned mood she thought it would be the very last time she could be in the West in her entire life.

Lost in thought, she reached Kreuzberg, one of the Turkish neighbourhoods in West Berlin. She stopped in front of an antique silver store and spotted a silver birdcage in the shop window. It was tiny—made to be worn on a necklace. There was an even tinier bird in it, sitting on a bar. She bought the necklace for me as a gift. When she gave it to me she told me that my father would soon return. She said that they'd never be able to leave the isolation of East Germany, but that, one day, I'd be leaving alone. If they had to stay forever, at least I should go and see the world outside the cage. I decided then and there that that little piece of jewellery would be my lucky charm. I would wear it as a symbol whenever I crossed the border.

In the fall of 1989 political change came. I was eighteen years old when the boundaries of the Eastern Bloc were pried open. All of a sudden it was possible for us to travel the world.

In the following years I visited many countries. Out of an inexplicable hesitation I didn't go to Canada. Maybe I shied away from my own expectations—which were, I figured, connected to the fantasies of that difficult time so many years ago.

I finally did make it, however. I am, like my parents, an artist, and a couple of years ago I was invited by another artist to an exhibit in Toronto. I remembered the lucky charm my mother had given me fifteen years earlier. I wore the birdcage on a silver ring in my ear when I passed the Canadian border control.

I had only twelve days to discover my "promised land." It was long enough for me to fall in love with a Canadian woman. She made me want to stay in your country forever. I did have to leave, on that twelfth day, but I left part of myself with her. As we said our goodbyes at the airport, I handed her the birdcage, hastily telling her the story.

In the past two years she has shown me much of Canada's beauty and introduced me to many wonderful Canadians. Modern Canada is different from the one I dreamt of as a child. But the Canada I love now is real.

Martin Weinhold

Berlin, Germany

TEACHING THE DANCER TO PULL

I was born on a farm in the Annapolis Valley in Nova Scotia. My father's parents shared their home with us. Their other son, my uncle Robbie, owned a similar property a short distance down the road. Since there was little money to buy farm equipment, the two brothers shared everything. Not only did they share implements and machinery, but they each contributed a horse to the team required to perform heavy tasks around the farms and woodlots.

Eventually my father took over my grandfather's farm. Grandfather had a carriage horse named Dick. In his youth, Dick had been a racehorse pacer. In his new career he was more suited to pulling the riding wagon or passenger sleigh than being hitched to a wagon tongue with a draught horse on the other side. When Dick saw an open road he had only one thought: run.

Down at the other farm, my uncle had Queenie and Gunner, a well-matched horse team. When Queenie died, Gunner needed a teammate. Out of necessity, Dick was put into a work harness.

The life of the speedster was about to change.

Gunner was a sturdy-legged, Canadian prairie boy. Because of his size and strength he'd previously worked as a draught horse in a logging camp. When my uncle returned home from the First World War he bought Gunner to work on his farm.

Those who served as teamster to the mismatched pair had to work hard to keep Dick in check. As a small girl, I recall standing in my grandmother's bedroom watching the horses haul hay, apples, firewood, logs, pit props, and whatever other loads they were asked to pull. As I watched I sensed Dick's impatience at his plight.

No one knows what my uncle's designation was in the army, but I assumed he'd been a gunner, and that that was the origin of his horse's name. However, my brother Ernie recently told me that originally Gunner had been trained by the military to pull field guns. The war ended before he was shipped overseas, so he escaped the horrors of France. His work in logging camps, even in harsh conditions, paled beside the life he would have experienced pulling heavy artillery in the muddy and bloody battlefields. The horse soldier now had much gentler battles to fight. One was the red Annapolis Valley clay that stuck to his hooves like glue when it rained, and the other was teaching Dick, the dancer, to pull.

Dawn Hembling
Ajax, Ontario

THE BIG MOVE

My neighbour Tommy Gordon has a philosophy that anything is possible if you have enough time and the cost is within reason. He's proved this on many occasions to those who've come to him with problems that seemed beyond fixing.

If you have something to be repaired, welded, rebuilt, manufactured, blown up, blown down, or blown out, Tom is your man. He comes from a long line of self-reliant thinkers; farmers like him have to be, to survive.

At a young age Tommy took up dynamiting as a means of ridding fields of tree roots. He soon moved to blowing down unwanted farm silos. This unusual talent gained him recognition far and wide. If there was a silo to come down in southwestern Ontario, Tom got a call.

He had the reputation of being able to fell a silo within inches of surrounding structures.

But of all the things Tom blew up, the most famous was certainly the project on Ron Forbes's farm.

Ron Forbes actually owned two farms that abutted the same concession. Ron's problem was that he had a fine silo on the south farm, but needed one on the north farm. He had to haul feed from the south silo to the north farm daily, and this constant trekking back and forth caused a good deal of wear and tear on his equipment. In the fall of 1993, after harvest when things were a little less hectic, Ron met with Tom. They came up with the idea of moving the silo from the south farm to the north farm—a distance of about three-quarters of a mile. And so the adventure began.

The only way to move this behemoth was to get it onto a sled and tow it across the concession. The first order of business was to ensure that nowhere en route was the elevation greater than eleven degrees—if it was, the silo would tip over. The proposed route met the requirement.

Next, the silo had to be jacked up, one side at a time. Enough to get a sled constructed under each side, but never more than the determined eleven degrees. The silo had to be cut through about two feet up from the base with a cement saw.

Tom travelled to a shipyard in Port Dover to get clevises and cable heavy enough to do the job. In conversation with the ship repair people, Tom was advised to put the cable around the silo rather than around the sled—otherwise, the sled was likely to be yanked out from beneath the silo.

That meant the silo had to be reinforced so that the pulling cable wouldn't crush it.

Finally the day came. The cables were attached. The sled was ready. Three bulldozers were fanned out with cables taut. The show was about to begin. Cars were lined up along the road and there was much argument as to whether or not Tom's plan would work. There was wagering as to if and when the silo would topple over. Tom stationed himself in front of the three bulldozers like the grandmaster of a parade, which, I suppose, in a way he was.

The actual move was a bit of a letdown as the dozers and silo moved without a hitch. Once it got going the whole procession moved at the pace of a good walk. There was a problem, however, in that there was no base to put the silo on at the destination site. Tom, Ron, and gang had been pretty sure they could pull it off but not sure enough to build the base, so everything stopped twenty feet short of home plate. A cement base was poured, but by the time it was ready it had rained a good deal. It was a muddy mess to move the silo the last twenty feet, but they got it done.

The silo-moving business is slow; nothing has come up since the big move. I would guess that every time Tom drives by the famous silo he gets a little twinge of satisfaction. As the years have passed by, the silo is no longer in use, so maybe someday Tom will get the call to come blow it down. But I hope it stays standing because it represents what can be done if you're positive and put your mind to it.

Carl Chambers

Woodstock, Ontario

THE RESCUE

One beautiful summer morning our dog, Lucky, and I went to check on our horses. The walk took us past our pond. In the summer the pond is surrounded by tall grass, so we often see wildlife. That morning was no exception.

Lucky had run ahead of me and, as he did, a deer stood up. The deer, which was a doe, stared at the dog and started moving toward it, head down. Clearly it was protecting something. It didn't take us long to figure out what. A small fawn jumped out from behind her mother and started running in the other direction, away from her mother and toward the pond. The doe, dog, and I watched in amazement as the little fawn dove into the pond headfirst. It didn't come up for ten or twelve feet. When it finally surfaced it started swimming for the other side of the pond.

I stood there astonished at how well the fawn could swim. It couldn't have been more than a few weeks old. But as I watched, I could see that it was getting weak. As the fawn neared my side of the pond I started thinking that I should grab it and pull it out. But as soon as it saw me standing there it panicked and headed back toward its mother on the opposite shore.

The fawn was now back in the middle of the pond and slowing down. It looked exhausted. When I saw it wasn't going to make it I started running toward the other shore. The fawn had made it to within ten feet of its mother. But all I could see was the top of its head.

At this point, what with me running and the dog barking, its mother had run off.

Without thinking I jumped into the pond and started pulling the fawn out. It wasn't much bigger than a cat, so it didn't take much. It was as limp as a dishrag and water was pouring out of its mouth and nose. I let the water drain and quickly put its whole muzzle into my mouth.

I had no idea what to do next.

So I blew into its muzzle for two seconds and then let the breath exhale. I did this for about twenty seconds, and all of a sudden one of the fawn's eyes shot open. It started coughing up water, and when it was done, it looked at me with both eyes. It wasn't panicked or scared, it just stared at me.

The fawn didn't seem to have any strength, but I knew it would be okay. I laid it down, back where it had been with its mother, and curled its body into a sopping wet ball. Its mother was nowhere to be seen, but I knew she wasn't far away, and she certainly wouldn't be coming any closer as long as I was on the scene.

Half an hour later I went back to check. The bed was empty.

I haven't seen either of them since.

Robert Sachno

Pierrepont, New York

ON THE SUNNY SIDE
OF THE STREET

I met Wray in the fall of 1998. My husband and I had just moved to Tecumseh, near Windsor, and were settling into our two-bedroom apartment. Wray's wife, Teddy, the more outgoing of the two, introduced herself to us in the elevator on moving day.

My husband responded by introducing us.

"This is my wife, Netty. My name is Brad."

"I know," said Teddy.

"What floor do you live on?" I asked her.

"The same one you're on," replied Teddy. "My husband, Wray, and I live just down the hall from you."

Apparently, news travelled quickly in this apartment building that was home to many seniors. A young couple in their mid-thirties moving into the building had prompted a flurry of excitement amongst the elderly residents.

"Well," I promised Teddy, "we'll have you over for tea once we settle in."

A few weeks later, Brad came home with a basket of plums that one of his parishioners had given him. I remembered my promise to Teddy and decided to invite our new neighbours over for tea and plum pie the following day.

The next afternoon we were sitting in our kitchen, empty dessert plates pushed to the centre of the table and with a second cup of tea in our hands. Conversation flowed freely between Teddy, Brad, and me. However, I was keen on involving Wray. So I began to ask him questions. His answers were limited to one or two words.

As time passed, I noticed Wray looking at the piano in our living room. I asked him if he played an instrument. At that, Wray's eyes lit up. He told me about his band, The Wray Chapman Orchestra. For three years, before World War II, Wray and his band played in the Sarnia-Glencoe area. He then left to serve his country as an operating room nurse in a front-line field hospital. After the war, Wray's love of music never faded. He played with different bands in the Windsor area. If he wasn't playing for audiences, he was playing for family and friends.

I asked Wray if he'd be interested in getting together occasionally to play. Again, his eyes lit up.

For the next year, Wray shuffled down the hall once a week to our apartment, music stand in one hand, guitar in the other, and a bundle of sheet music under his arm. I would meet this eighty-two-year-old halfway, taking his music stand in my one hand and his arm in my other. As we made our way back to my apartment, I'd listen to him outline the repertoire for our afternoon session. We would then settle in for the next hour, allowing the music to flow out of our hearts, me on piano and Wray on guitar.

In 1999 my husband and I purchased a home and left Wray and Teddy at the apartment in Tecumseh. We kept in touch and, over the years, witnessed a decline in Wray's health. In December 2001 we visited Wray in the hospital before leaving for Montreal, where Brad could complete some courses at Presbyterian College.

Brad said to me as we left Wray's hospital room, "You'd better take one more look at your friend—it might be the last time you see him."

It was.

We received a call from Wray's family a few weeks later. We went home, and on February 20th, Brad assisted at Wray's memorial service and I played Wray's and my favourite song, "On the Sunny Side of the Street," alone.

It was one of the hardest things I've ever had to do.

Netty Watson
Windsor, Ontario

DISCOVERING DIEPPE

Recently my fiancée, Lynsay, and I went on a vacation to France. We took the opportunity to visit the beaches of Normandy. Our destination was the city of Dieppe and the Canadian World War II cemetery. Neither Lynsay nor I had lost family there; in fact, between the two of us, only Lynsay's grandfathers had fought and lived through the war. We're pretty fortunate, and we know it, which is part of why we felt compelled to visit the cemetery that day.

We drove into the seaside town and toward the water, expecting the scene of the great military landing to be the logical location of the burial ground. And, sure enough, when we reached the sea, parked the car, and walked up to the rock-filled beaches, we spotted a Canadian flag. A lump formed in my throat.

"Here we are," I announced. Unfortunately, what we'd found was a seaside casino with a set of international flags. Where was this world-famous cemetery? we wondered.

Dieppe is a factory town. Most of the people there felt pretty intimidating for an English-speaking couple from downtown

Toronto. But, in our best and admittedly rusty Canadian French, we inquired about the location of the cemetery.

"Ou est le cimetière des Canadiens?"

Much to our dismay, none of the locals seemed to know. Most of them kept pointing away from the water and saying something about a nearby town.

Back in the car, we drove around Dieppe for over two hours, growing increasingly frustrated with each dead end.

Finally, in the middle of a roundabout, we spotted a small green sign. We followed it and a series of others that led us out of the actual city of Dieppe and into a farming community some miles away. And there, in amongst roaming fields filled with thick, fragrant poppies, lay a small cemetery with a simple stone-arch entrance. We parked at the end of a dead-end country road and walked inside the cemetery.

We were alone, looking out at rows upon rows of rectangular white monuments—each as straight as a line of soldiers in formation. The grass was freshly trimmed. The grounds smelled of moist greenery. It was like nothing I'd ever experienced. At each grave there was a flower, laid with military precision, yet the decoration was so sublime and fair you'd think the invisible groundskeeper was an artist.

As we examined each gravestone, Lynsay remarked on the large number of deceased who hailed from her hometown of Hamilton, that most of the men were really just boys, and that most of the deaths had taken place over a three-day period. "There must be a thousand young men buried here," she said.

My thoughts were abruptly interrupted by the sound of a woman yelling in French and honking her car horn. I walked to the entrance to find a rugged, middle-aged woman, a local, waving something in her hand.

As it happens, I must have been so excited to have found the cemetery that when I exited my car I'd dropped, in the middle of the road, my brown leather dossier containing our passports and all our money for our trip—about eight hundred euros. The French woman was honking her horn so that she could return my case.

As the woman made a hasty retreat to her beat-up, twenty-year-old Peugeot, I called out, "Thank you, thank you! *Merci.*" She shook her head, looked me in the eye—and then at the graveyard—and said, *"Non, non. Merci."* She was pointing at me.

It took me a moment to realize what she was trying to say.

After she left, I examined the dossier and saw that the case had been opened, but not a penny or passport was missing. She'd seen that we were Canadian, and although I'm sure that money could have solved a whole bunch of her problems, she felt compelled to return it.

So, as we discovered, the people of Dieppe haven't forgotten what some very brave Canadians did, so long ago—they just chose simple gestures of kindness to express their gratitude.

Tyler Levine
Toronto, Ontario

PICNIC, POSTPONED

This story begins when I started working at the Safeway grocery store in Richmond, British Columbia. I worked in the deli for many years. Over those years I became friends with a sandy-haired, fast-moving customer.

He always arrived on Saturday morning with a list an arm long. He moved quickly, and was in and out of the store before you knew it, whistling classical music and going his merry way.

Over the years, we started chatting. He would stop at my deli counter and stay just a bit longer each week.

I learned that he worked for CP Air. That he had a family of five. And that he lived just around the corner. Our over-the-counter chit-chat became a ritual, and we had some good laughs. He called me his "baloney-salami Saturday psychiatrist."

I can't remember how the idea of a picnic came about, but somehow it did. Every week we would make plans—pretend dates—to meet at places like Garry Point Park. The deal was I would bring the baloney and he would bring the homemade wine. It was all in jest, but it was fun. And each Saturday morning we'd talk about why we had each "forgotten" to show up.

Sometimes his wife would come with him to the store, and she and I would have a laugh about her husband and me never making our picnic "date."

Years went by. And every week we played this game. Once I told him that I couldn't sell him a barbecue chicken. I said I felt he wasn't responsible enough to look after a dead bird. He agreed.

We must have been about the same age—around fifty-five— so I noticed, with concern, when his step became slow and he lost so much weight. I also noticed that he rarely whistled anymore.

I wanted to ask him, but I knew that wouldn't be right; he was a customer. His wife started to shop more often. I felt a cloud hanging over both of them. One day when she came in I could see that she was crying. After serving her at the deli I asked my manager if I could take my break. I walked with the man's wife out to the parking lot. She told me that my "never-to-have-a-picnic friend" was dying of cancer in Richmond Hospital. We hugged and cried.

Then she looked up at me and said, "You guys never made it to the picnic."

I asked her if I could make up a picnic basket for the three of us and bring it to the hospital that night. She agreed. I packed soda crackers, yogurt, and bananas. She'd told me those were the only things he could swallow.

From her husband's chit-chat, I knew that her favourite

sandwich was Italian salami with Swiss cheese on a kaiser bun. We had wine for the ladies, candles, and a red-and-white-checkered tablecloth.

The nurse was kind enough to close the room-divider curtains. We had a window looking out on the park. We laughed and cried together as they told me about their children, and the struggles of their life.

After twenty-five years we were finally getting to know each other. We finally got our long-overdue picnic.

Our time together was short, as my customer grew tired quickly. His sandy hair was gone and the fast-moving body was now almost lifeless. We said our goodbyes. I knew I would never see him again.

He fought hard, but a few weeks later he could fight no longer.

I made the sandwich trays for his funeral with fond memories of the times we spent over the counter. It didn't matter that I didn't know his name; we knew each other as people. That's what was important.

Margreth Fry
Richmond, British Columbia

YEAR
SEVEN

AIR MAIL

2C POSTAGE 2C

DOGGING SATURN

My son is a bit of a junior astronomer. He's got this big, honking telescope that looks like something out of NASA. He pores over sky maps and plots the movement of celestial bodies. A cloudy evening can really bring him down.

The kid loves space. He talks about space endlessly and uses words I've never heard of and concepts I don't understand. I'm always asked to look at pictures of nebulae and to ponder along with him about things like black holes.

He likes to show me his finds too, through his telescope. And I like that. I've seen the moon in all its phases. There's something huge about the contrast of light and shadow on the moon that makes you hold your breath for just a second.

Lately, he's been dogging Saturn.

"It's in our sky now," he says. More sky maps. More searching. More looking thoughtfully out the windows into the sky. Sometimes I worry that maybe he's really looking for the planet that he came from. Ian, phone home.

So, then he needed a compass. South by southeast. That's where Saturn was. He needs the compass to find his way. When could we get one? Well, he had a day off school and spent all of it helping me in the library where I work. He shelved books and did endless tedious chores on the computer. I figured it was a good day to do something for him, so we went to Mountain Equipment Co-op after work.

The guy at the store was just like all the others there: healthy, vigorous, outdoor-loving. He was enthused when he found out we were looking for a compass.

"What's it for? Orienteering? Map work?"

I couldn't resist.

"He needs it to find Saturn," I said, indicating Ian beside me.

"Astronomy! Cool!" he said, turning to Ian, and I became the dork once again. The two of them pored over the compasses, selecting the right one for Ian. He fussed with it all the way home, advising me of my exact bearings.

At 10 p.m., when I was tucked into bed, there was a knock at my door.

"Come and see this," he said. So, I went. He pointed to the telescope and I looked.

"It's Saturn. Can you see it?"

You know what? I *could* see it. I could. It was Saturn, unmistakably so. From my living room window, there between the branches of the big basswood tree, south by southeast, was Saturn. And I felt profoundly good. I could have stepped away from the telescope and pointed into the sky directly at Saturn and known it was right there even though I couldn't see it. And there is comfort in that.

The world is big ... and bigger still if, like Ian, you want it to include the black holes, and the nebulae, and Saturn. But it's also right there. Right there beside you, or right there worlds beyond where your finger can point. It doesn't matter. If you use the maps and record the findings, it's right there.

Leah Sweetland

Winnipeg, Manitoba

MEETING THE QUEEN

Our first home, after our marriage in 1975, was a third-floor apartment on Sherbrooke Street in Montreal.

This was at a time when English organizations in Montreal were beginning to realize that it was an asset to have bilingual employees.

My husband and I, having grown up in English-speaking neighbourhoods, had never made much use of the French skills we had acquired in school. Now that I was actually beginning to use French in my daily life, I was keen to practise.

So I was excited to find that the name of the concierge in our apartment building was Alphonse Fournier. Alphonse took it upon himself to teach us newlyweds about much more than French language and culture. He acquainted us with various aspects of car maintenance, laundry, cleaning, snow removal, and pressure cookers. Pressure cookers, he told us, could destroy a marriage!

One day when I delivered our rent cheque to Alphonse's apartment I noticed a collection of newspaper clippings taped to the wall behind him. All of them contained photographs of Her Majesty, the Queen. The pictures of British royalty in Alphonse's home surprised me. I commented on them.

Alphonse's response surprised me even more.

Pointing to his collection, he said, "I've met her. And I like her."

In answer to my "how, when, and where" questions, Alphonse told me the following story:

During World War II he left his Gaspé home to serve with the Canadian Army. Eventually he ended up as the head of a convoy in the south of England.

One day he was travelling down the road when he noticed another military vehicle at the side of the road. He signalled for his convoy to stop so that they could offer help.

Alphonse said, "As I got closer I realized that it was HER."

He'd come upon Princess Elizabeth, then a member of the Women's Auxiliary Corps.

She'd been driving with another woman in the corps. Their vehicle had broken down. Alphonse offered to attempt to fix the problem, and suggested to the two women that they might wish to sit down nearby. Two things impressed him and caused him to become emotional as he told me the story. First, he said, the Princess had immediately responded to him in French. Second, she'd said she would remain standing because Alphonse was a higher rank than she was.

And that is how one of the Princess's (and later, the Queen's) most ardent admirers was born.

Alphonse's story comes to my mind whenever I think about the importance of respecting everyone we encounter along the path of life.

Janet Chandler Allingham
Morrisburg, Ontario

MARY'S PIANO

About eighteen years ago I bought a baby grand piano from a woman in Langley, British Columbia. A Heintzman. Ten years later I called the woman, Mary Dumbleton, to tell her how much my daughter and I were enjoying the piano. We both played it every day. We'd nicknamed it "Mary" in her honour.

Mary told me a little bit about the history of the piano and how it had come to be in her family. She thanked me for calling, and suggested that maybe we could get together someday.

In May of this year I read in the *Vancouver Sun* that Mary Dumbleton of Langley, B.C., had passed away, "loved and deeply mourned."

I felt saddened by this, and recalled something she'd told me in our phone conversation, so I decided to send a condolence card to her family via her home address. The card explained who I was, and that I was sorry to read that their mom had passed away. It also said that Mary had told me her family had always been a little resentful that she'd sold the piano, and if they wanted to replace *my* piano I'd be happy to return the little Heintzman to the Dumbleton family.

I sent this card off and waited for the family's reply.

About a week later I came home and found a note on the counter, written in my husband's hand.

The note said:

Mary Dumbleton called.

I was stunned. The only thing I could think of when I read those words was "How is this possible? Where could she be calling from?"

I called my husband at work and asked him.

"Mary Dumbleton called? What did she say?"

"She said she liked the card," he told me. He didn't know what I'd done.

"She said she liked the card?" I asked.

"Yeah, we had a nice chat."

I waited a week before I got up the nerve to call her and tell her how happy I was that she was still alive. We both had a good laugh about it. She said that it was a lovely sentiment but that she'd be happy if the piano stayed where it was. She thanked me for calling. She said maybe we could get together someday. She said maybe she could visit me in Horseshoe Bay and see her namesake.

I look forward to that day. And send condolences to the family of the *other* Mary Dumbleton of Langley, B.C.

Jerry Mills
Horseshoe Bay, British Columbia

TWICE IN A LIFETIME

On a cold January evening three years ago, on a snowy street corner in North Toronto, I suffered what the medical professionals call a "sudden witnessed collapse." I remember virtually nothing of the day itself, and certainly nothing of the next few, some of which I spent in a drug-induced coma packed on ice, "like a flounder," as my wife would say. But, a double bypass and three months' recuperation later, I was pretty much back to normal, albeit twenty-five pounds lighter and on a much healthier diet and exercise regime.

The survival rate for such incidents is less than ten percent. I wanted to meet and thank the people who'd responded that day: the firefighters and paramedics who brought me back from a "vital signs absent" state. Over the next few months, I did just that. A family connection in the fire department put me in touch with the crew, and my wife and I visited them at their fire hall. Getting to the paramedics was more difficult, but eventually I met them too, and learned more about what had happened that day, and just how close I'd come to death. Their reaction was well summed up by one of the firefighters, who said, "So often I go home and tell my wife about something like this, but we never know how it turns out. It's great to see that this had a happy ending."

But there was one big hole in the story. Who was the witness to my "sudden witnessed collapse"? All we knew was that a woman saw me fall into a snowbank, called 911, and stayed with me until the emergency crews arrived. However, as far as we could tell, no one had taken her name, and we couldn't think of any practical way of finding her.

Last winter we decided to take up ballroom dancing, which meant that once a week I'd meet my wife at the children's bookstore where she works, where in fact I was headed on the night of my episode. I don't visit the store all that often, and usually stay for only a few minutes. I walked into the store wearing a coat very similar to the one from two years earlier, and the same hat. Just inside the door, a woman was looking at a book display. She glanced up at me as I stepped past her.

"Excuse me," she said, "may I ask you a personal question?"

I stopped and looked at her, trying to figure out where we could have met.

Then she said, "Did you have a heart attack near here about two years ago?"

"Yes, I did," I said.

"Well," she said, "I'm the person who was there that night."

My angel, as it turns out, is named Helen Healy. She'd changed her plans that evening and was heading home when I passed her, looking, she said, "like a man in a big hurry." She told me that when I was about fifty paces ahead of her, I staggered, grabbed at a bus-stop pole, then collapsed. She quickly reached me, saw I was unconscious, and dialed 911. Incredibly, she said, although there was bumper-to-bumper rush-hour traffic just a few feet away, no one stopped. She pointed to my dark cap, the same one I was wearing that night, and said, "You have to get rid of that and get a red one. If I hadn't been there, no one would have seen you."

She'd started CPR, but, as she noted, I'm a big man and she's a small woman, and after a while she saw I was slipping away. The dispatcher told her that the ambulance was only a minute away. At that point, she said, she stopped the CPR and gave me a big hug.

"Hang on," she'd said, "don't die on me."

Moments later, the emergency crews arrived and took over.

Helen and I had the same sense that while our first meeting was fortunate, our second one was miraculous. Even now I can't accurately describe my feelings as we stood there talking. I told her, hoping not to sound ungrateful, that I needed some time to sort out my reactions. Later, she told me that she'd found it "emotionally unsettling."

We remain amazed at the coincidences that caused our paths to cross not once, but twice, on two snowy January evenings.

Jim Cowan
Toronto, Ontario

SPIT BUGS

I was looking at my to-do list today. You know the one: posted in command central, the place where you can find plenty of loathsome tasks waiting for your attention.

Our lists are posted on a big whiteboard in our kitchen. Most of them written in my wife's careful script.

But the list I was looking at today was written in my own hand. Yes, I'd broken the sacred rule and added to my husbandly burden. Mind you, in my defence, it was obvious that I'd made this error sometime in the exuberant throes of spring, and, to the best of my knowledge, had yet to act on any of the items. Now I was standing in front of it, coffee in hand, ready to erase it.

But when I reread the list, rather than erasing it I drew a black border around it and framed it instead. It's not that it's a significant list. It seems that when I wrote it I had need of lumber for a long-forgotten project. And that I was thinking sticks might make good perches for the birds in our garden. And that evidently it was berry season: we were having, as I recall, a "spittle bug" problem in one of our shrubs.

It was the sum of these things that made me smile. As I

stood gazing at it, I thought, "This is a good list. This list is too good to erase."

So I left it where it was, in the corner of our whiteboard, the frame around it. And if I ever feel that there's nothing to do, or that I have no purpose in life, it's there for me to consult. Life could be worse.

Here then is my permanent to-do list:

Get Wood
Find Big Sticks
Pick Strawberries
Spit Bugs

Paul Jensen

Ottawa, Ontario

CULTURE OF KINDNESS

Our father has Alzheimer's disease. It's been creeping up on him for the last ten years like a slowly rising tide. Finally my mother realized that she had to put him in residential care.

The first place that took Dad was a hospital that accepted dementia patients. Despite that custom, it seemed they never knew what to do with him. Every week there was a complaint about his behaviour. He lost weight so rapidly that the social worker there suspected they were forgetting to take him to the dining room to eat. Within two months he had pneumonia and was obviously deeply disoriented and unhappy.

Fortunately, a bed became available at the Lodge at Broadmead, a veterans' residence in Victoria. The contrast was immediately apparent. While both locations had small rooms, and hospital beds, and private gardens, and activities for residents, the atmosphere at Broadmead was cheerful and homey. The staff had obviously been hired for their skill, compassion, and patience, and were thoroughly trained in handling Alzheimer's patients. From the beginning, I noticed that the culture was one of kindness, not bureaucracy or efficiency.

What I found particularly wonderful were the events that broke the monotony of the residents' lives. While there are a number of activities throughout the day, once a week each unit in Broadmead gets a visit from Ania, the art therapist. Ania brings everyone who's able, or willing, up to the large, bright art room and gets them going on their projects. The crafts they make are sold in the gift shop, which defrays the cost of supplies.

Dad had been a truly talented amateur artist, taking up pastels in his retirement with the same attention to order and detail he'd brought to his lifelong career in the military. Once Alzheimer's stole his capabilities, I tried to get him interested in his pastels, but he didn't remember them and resisted my invitations to try them out.

It was Ania who got him painting again. Not only on his designated day, but every morning.

And slowly Dad transformed. Now, at eighty-nine, he's no longer restless and grumpy or visibly frightened. He seems quietly content. And while his mind doesn't remember, I believe his body knows that he's both well treated and well loved.

On one of my visits I saw Dad in the art room, concentrating on a length of silk. It was stretched over a board on which there were three evenly spaced knobs. The silk was tied tightly over the knobs.

"Ahhh," I said to myself, "Dad's going to do tie-dye. How very much like him to do something with military precision."

I thought no more of it until, during one of my daily phone chats with my mother, she said, "Your father painted a scarf. They entered it in the Saanich Fair, and it won first prize."

So I wept. I wept knowing that he wouldn't remember painting it—even if he saw it. And that he wouldn't remember winning—no matter how many times he was told. I wept with deep gratitude for this wonderful place and the people who understand about love, and fun, and capability, and dignity long past remembering.

My mother bought the scarf from the gift shop and gave it to me for my birthday. I wore it the last time I visited Dad.

He admired it.

Ann Perodeau
Calgary, Alberta

FREUDIAN SLIP

One spring day a few years ago, my wife and I went for a drive.

The wind was blustery. But we didn't care about the wind. We wanted to see the town. We wanted to say hello to it after a long winter. We wanted to *smell* the air and *feel* the wind. So we rode with all the windows open, with no radio on, and with little conversation. Our conversation was the pleasure of each other's company.

The one drawback was the layer of winter sand on the roads. It was dry, and the wind was blowing the sand into the air and into many swirling dust devils.

As we turned the corner onto one of the side streets near the college, we noticed two college-age girls walking together along the road. They were also enjoying the day in their light spring dresses, talking and laughing together. And *that* was the fateful moment when two things happened at precisely the same time.

The first was that a particularly strong blast of wind blew past the girls and caught the hems of their dresses so that they both had to do a quick Marilyn Monroe stance.

I thought to myself, "If that wind had been moving just a

little faster it would have blown those dresses clean up over their heads." I promise, Stuart, there was no wishing involved.

At the same moment, a gust of wind—doubtless the same mischievous gust that had ruffled the girls' dresses—blew dust into the car through my wife's window and into my eyes. Another thought entered my brain: "Now would be a good time for my wife to roll up her window." Those two thoughts met in my brain like young lovers at a garden party.

Rubbing my eyes, I asked my wife, "Honey, would you please roll up your dress?"

She wasn't wearing a dress, Stuart. Those two girls—they were wearing dresses.

All I was able to do was drop my jaw and croak out some guttural grunting groans. By rights, my wife should have cuffed me. But instead she smiled, and broke out laughing. I pulled the car over and we laughed together. That there, Mr. McLean, is a fine example of a woman with a sense of humour.

A.J. Mittendorf

Prince George, British Columbia

BIRD DOG

There is a common belief that if you touch a bird's nest, or the eggs within it, or, heaven forbid, the tiny birds that emerge from those eggs, that little bit of life will not survive. The parent birds will never return, so the rule goes, after a human hand has touched the nest.

I'm not sure this is true.

Every spring a bird builds its nest in the clematis that drapes over our front stoop. From a bird's point of view, this is probably like buying the cutest little bungalow in the dodgiest area of town. While the entryway to our home is framed by pale flowers falling like a pink waterfall, the nests built here have inevitably fallen prey to the neighbourhood gang of crows. So that year, when I once again discovered a tiny sparrow's nest perched in the clematis, my heart sank a little. Dumb birds, I thought.

Just the same, the miracle of a nest captured my imagination. Every day I'd watch the to and fro of the birds, and then secretly peek in on the nest to see—first, four impossibly tiny eggs, and then four dandelion-like fuzz balls with beaks. It was a wonder.

But the predictable happened. One day, as I prepared a snack for our five-year-old son, Dean, we heard the cacophony of cawing crows and shrieking sparrows. I raced out the front door with a pot in hand to scare the vandals off. But as we looked up at the nest we saw a crow swooping into the sky, a chunk of the nest trailing from its mouth. I was too late.

"It's the natural way," I cautioned myself, trying not to become too sentimental about this heart-wrenching event. Little Dean, much closer to the ground than I, suddenly pointed out, "There's a bird!" And, indeed, there *was* a tiny bird. A miniature feathered dinosaur, sitting on the grass, dumped from its nest in the raid. And then we found another and then another. Three tiny birds, untouched by the predator crow. Only one had become lunch. The remaining small sparrows appeared unharmed by their near-death experience.

As I sadly reflected on the fate of the fourth sparrow, my glance settled on our old dog, Mica. Mica's nose was angled downward toward the ground while her eyes were cast upward toward Dean and me. She looked guilty—there's just no other way to describe that expression. Two little sticks poked out of her mouth.

But wait. They weren't sticks. They were *legs*. Bird legs!

"Drop that bird!" I commanded. Mica's obedience-school days were long behind her, but my tone must have communicated something, because that dog slowly, reluctantly, spat out Bird Number Four. Expecting the worst, I gathered up the tiny body in my palm. The sparrow was perfectly fine—just a bit wet.

Little Dean and I quickly reconstructed the busted nest,

using some cotton batting and a few well-placed branches. We set all four little birds back into their renovated home.

And we waited.

I must admit that I worried we might have condemned those small creatures to a more grisly death in that nest than if we'd left them on the ground for the next cat that passed by. But by dinnertime the parents were back, busy feeding their hungry brood.

That family of birds survived and left the nest on their own accord.

Sometimes things work out just as you hope.

Maureen Koch

Victoria, British Columbia

STANDING, PROUDLY

This story takes place twenty-five years ago, at the beginning of my public service career. I was working in Calgary for the federal government, interviewing immigrants who were applying for Canadian citizenship. It was a job that reminded me, every day, how lucky I was to be born in this great country.

During my four years, I met many courageous people from around the world who had sacrificed so much to come to Canada. There's one family that I think of often.

In the early 1980s, many of the "boat people" from Vietnam had spent enough time in Canada to qualify for citizenship. One day I interviewed a young Vietnamese woman who wanted help for her father. He was in the hospital. He was dying, and he didn't want to die stateless and be buried as a refugee. He didn't want to die without a country to call home.

Time was short. Could we help?

I'm proud to say that we did. We pulled out all the stops to get the paperwork processed quickly, and then we arranged to go to the hospital to give this man the gift of belonging.

When we arrived at the cancer ward of the Foothills Hospital, we were greeted by a nurse who told us that our soon-to-be citizen was a very proud man. He was not about to become a Canadian while lying in bed. He'd struggled into a wheelchair and was in the lounge waiting for us. Well, that wasn't all that was waiting for us. The nurses had decorated the lounge in red and white: streamers, balloons, flags. Patients from the ward, all dressed in hospital garb, had crowded into the room. The citizenship judge said a few words, administered the oath of citizenship, and presented the much-cherished certificate.

And then a young man standing in the back, bald from chemo and hanging on to his IV pole, started to sing "O Canada." One by one the people in the room joined in. By the second verse, everyone in the room was belting out the national anthem.

I often take for granted the life I have here in Canada. I complain about small things. But when I catch myself doing it I think back to that man in the hospital and the hundreds of other people whom I had the privilege of meeting. And when I do, I thank my lucky stars.

Colette Arnal
Ottawa, Ontario

BIRTHDAY SUIT

Our family has always enjoyed camping. My husband and I tented on our honeymoon twenty-six years ago. We upgraded to a hard-top camper when we had kids. Then, about fifteen years ago, we opted for total luxury: a twenty-four-foot travel trailer with a pullout couch for us at the front and bunk beds in the back for our children.

We were on our maiden voyage with the new rig at one of our favourite campgrounds. It was Canada Day weekend. We were lucky to get a spot.

We were located right across from the tents and trailers occupied by the young campground staff. Summer holidays had arrived.

We were enjoying the time together as a family and the conveniences of our little home on wheels. Life was good. We were still campers, just a little less rugged. We still hadn't caught on to locking the door.

One night I was awakened in the wee hours of the morning by my husband's voice saying, "This isn't your trailer."

In my sleepy state I thought to myself, "Well of course it's my trailer ... what's yours is mine and what's mine is ... mine."

Then I opened my eyes.

There was a young man standing next to our bed, an inebriated young man. A naked, inebriated young man. My husband was trying to direct him to the door, telling him that it wasn't his trailer.

After a few minutes of discussion our intruder left. We quickly locked the door.

Our eight-year-old son had slept through the whole event, but not our five-year-old daughter. A little voice from behind the curtains near the bunk beds called out, "Is he gone?"

In my most reassuring mother's voice I told her, "He's gone, you don't have to be afraid."

She said, "I'm not afraid. I just didn't want to miss anything."

Then she asked, "What happened?"

Since she'd been shielded by a curtain I tried to explain as best I could. I told her that the man had made a mistake and come into our trailer because he was, well, ah ... "sleep-walking."

After a moment's thought she asked, "Did he have his arms out in front of him?"

"No," I replied, "not his arms."

In the morning a sober and embarrassed young man came over to apologize. He explained that he'd celebrated his birthday a bit too much and had become disoriented when he wandered out of his trailer in the middle of the night. I told him I'd known it was his birthday by what he was wearing.

As we parted on good terms he said he hoped that someday

I'd be able to laugh about the incident. Well, that day did come, very quickly, and this story continues to be our camping favourite.

Dawn DeCourcey
Fredericton, New Brunswick

BY AIR MAIL
PAR AVION

YEAR EIGHT

A PROPOSAL
OF HOPE

In movies and on television, whenever someone meets a married couple, it seems—or at least it seems to me—the question "How did he propose?" comes up. Fifteen years ago I proposed to the woman I loved. But in fifteen years, not one person has ever asked the story of how I popped the question. Being a typical American, despite not being asked I'm going to tell the story anyway: not because I'm full of myself, but because I think it's a good story.

In September of 1996, my lovely girlfriend, Kim, and I had just graduated from college. We'd both studied biology and were making plans for graduate school. We had the world at our feet. Our grand plans came to an abrupt and unpleasant halt when Kim was diagnosed with leukemia. I don't think I need to elaborate on what a diagnosis like that can do to a twenty-two-year-old who thought she was just beginning her life as an adult.

Kim immediately began receiving treatments, which at times felt more dangerous than the disease itself. For the next six months she spent over half her time in the hospital, stuck on the cancer floor. Kim very rarely complained about her condition or her circumstances. She was the doctors' and nurses' favourite patient. The most heartbreaking one, too.

I spent those six months driving to the hospital, sitting by her bed, watching TV with her, and pacing the halls. And I worried about her. Whether it was denial or stubbornness or pigheadedness I'll never know, but I had a deep belief that she'd be all right.

Unfortunately, that belief wasn't shared by her physicians. After three aggressive rounds of chemotherapy, the leukemia kept coming back. The treatment wasn't working. Kim needed a bone marrow transplant, but a donor hadn't been found. Time was running out.

When the disease came back the fourth time, Kim was hospitalized for more chemotherapy. Her father caught me on my way into the hospital one day and took me to a waiting room. Looking exhausted and defeated, he shared dire news: Kim's physician didn't believe she would survive this fourth round of chemotherapy. She needed the transplant now.

He suggested we all prepare for the worst.

I sat back in the chair, stunned. My deep belief that Kim would be fine didn't jibe with this news. I looked at Kim's father and repeated that time-worn phrase many men have uttered before me: "Sir," I said, "I would like to ask for your daughter's hand in marriage."

Kim's father, being the big, strong, macho man that he is, immediately began to cry. I'm not sure what he was thinking, but I can only assume he felt some relief that his daughter would have a little happiness in all the gloom.

The next morning my mother took me to the jeweller where she and my father had bought their wedding rings. My mother, the jeweller, and the jeweller's wife spent hours with me finding just the right one.

That afternoon I began the hour-long drive to the hospital, practising the perfect speech. My heart was racing and my hands were shaky. When I entered Kim's room, my heart fell. She was sitting by the window, crying. This was not something she did often.

When I asked her what was wrong, she said that the case manager had just left. The case manager had shared the opinion of the medical staff with her: the end was near.

I went over to my jacket and pulled the small box from my pocket. I walked back to the chair she was sitting in, knelt down beside her, and gave her the little box.

I took off the surgical mask I was wearing, that was meant to protect her from my germs. I looked deeply into her eyes and said, "I believe in you."

So much for my practised oratory.

When she opened the box, Kim began crying all over again. But this time, just like her father, the tears were mingled with smiles and laughter. For the first time in what felt like ages, we kissed. The nursing staff discovered our happy news within about a nanosecond. Joy, which was not a common emotion on their floor, spread through the unit.

I'd like to be able to tell you that everything worked out okay. That a donor for Kim was found. That she got her transplant. That she got better. That we married, went to graduate school, bought a house, and started a family.

So I will. Because that's exactly what happened.

When looking back at that time in our lives, some folks like to say that Kim's survival and recovery was due to divine intervention, the result of some unimaginable number of prayers said and whispered on her behalf. I mean no disrespect to anyone, divine or otherwise, but I politely disagree.

I believe the turning point had more to do with that modest, pretty ring than anything else. Not because of me or what I did or didn't do, but because of what that little ring represented: hope.

Michael Gallagher

Hope, Maine

NIGHTCRAWLER

In grade two, my beloved teacher Mrs. Hossack taught the class a unit on worms. We read *How to Eat Fried Worms* by Thomas Rockwell. We wrote a story about a construction-paper worm that coiled around the classroom and out into the lobby. We made worms out of clay. My creation, a Cyndi Lauper worm with a red beehive and red lipstick, still sits on my father's desk.

One of our final tasks was to keep worms as pets in the classroom. Finding a worm to bring into class was delegated to my father; I was too squeamish to dig for it myself. And so, one Sunday night, there was my father, hunting through the grass in our side yard, flashlight in hand, worm hunting.

I have no doubt he did his share of grumbling while he was out in the dark, getting mud under his fingernails and a crick in his neck, all in the name of primary education.

He was probably remembering the many other times he'd "volunteered" his services—adopting the classroom gerbils during the previous summer, playing the Sultan during our dance studio's production of *Aladdin*. He might have been thinking how thankless a job being a father is and hoping I'd appreciate him more when I was older. Most of all, he would have wanted to get back inside where it was warm and dry so he could put his feet up and watch some TV with my mother before bed.

He was probably thinking all of these things when the police cruiser rolled by.

The officer slowed down when he saw the suspicious-looking flashlight moving in the dark. He turned on the strobe light, made a U-turn, and pulled up at the sidewalk. My father felt a brief moment of panic. He realized what he looked like, skulking around on someone's property in the middle of the night. Painted in the cruiser's red and blue lights, he felt like a criminal.

The officer stepped out of the car and strolled toward my father, who was desperately trying to figure out the simplest way to explain what he was doing without embarrassing himself. Before he could say anything, the officer spoke.

"Looking for worms?"

Apparently fathers all over the neighbourhood were out worm hunting that night.

I hope their children are as grateful for their dads as I am for mine.

Karyn Walmark

Mississauga, Ontario

A CATHEDRAL
OF FENCE POSTS

As a Canadian Forces chaplain, one of the more pleasant duties I perform is officiating at weddings.

I've had only two rules to guide me in which weddings I do and which I turn down: I need to be able to meet with the bride and groom first, and I don't do weddings in unusual places (like parachuting or underwater).

I broke both rules once, and it was the most meaningful wedding I've ever celebrated.

I'd agreed to do this wedding on two days' notice, as the minister who was to officiate was called away on a family emergency. I had the location (out of town, on a farm), I knew the names of the bride and groom, and I knew that they'd completed pre-marriage classes with the other minister.

I also knew something about their wedding guests and the particular setting they'd chosen for the celebration of their union. One hundred and forty bikers had come to spend the weekend. The wedding was to be a bonus—a surprise to all but a handful of the guests.

I confess to misgivings as I turned off the highway onto the property and caught my first glimpse of the venue. Dozens of motorcycles were parked in one section of the field. Most were Harley-Davidsons. Loud music filled the air from a refreshment area in the centre field. Tents dotted the landscape. It looked like a heavy-metal Woodstock.

Mine was the only Jetta in sight. I parked it and headed up to the house.

To my relief, things seemed to be in order. I was introduced to the bride's parents and the groom's parents while the bride was getting dressed. It didn't take long: she wore jeans and a black T-shirt and a few flowers in her hair. The groom was introduced to me as "Bear." It wasn't hard to know where the nickname came from—Bear outweighed me at least two to one. His beard was thick and bushy. His arms were heavily tattooed.

We checked to see that the licence was in order, and when everything was ready I headed to the main tent. I don't push through crowds very well, meek and mild sort that I am, but I managed to get to the front and asked for a microphone. I waited for the music to stop, introduced myself, and announced that I was here for a wedding. I wasn't sure what kind of reaction I would get.

Several of the bikers immediately headed to the parking area. The air was filled with the throb of powerful engines revving. Then, with almost military precision, the bikes pulled out and streamed toward the centre field. They were heading toward me. A few feet away, they turned off to form a double row facing each other—an honour guard to create an aisle for the bride. With engines at full throttle, their roar echoed across the valley.

As the bride walked slowly and gracefully down this aisle, each bike she passed switched off its engine. As she passed the last pair and all the engines were stilled, you could have heard a pin drop. She walked shyly up to Bear.

His eyes were overflowing with tears.

The couple were surrounded by a congregation of friends: members and families of the Sober Riders, each one a recovering alcoholic, each one a biker. Each one bowed in prayer as we entered a holy moment.

The bride had given me only one instruction for the service. "Make sure you have a sermon," she said. "These people want to hear a word from God."

I stood in the middle of the field, in a congregation of T-shirts, jeans, and tattoos, in front of a groom and bride who knew exactly what they were doing and why, in a cathedral of fence posts and Harleys, and together we gave thanks to God.

Neil Parker

Courtenay, British Columbia

PLUS ONE

In May 1975, I was a young, single Foreign Service officer who'd just been assigned to the Canadian Embassy in Japan. Shortly after my arrival in Tokyo, Queen Elizabeth and Prince Philip paid a state visit of five days to the Land of the Rising Sun.

In celebration of this momentous occasion, members of the Commonwealth were invited to a party in Shinjuku Garden to meet the Queen and the Prince. When my official invitation arrived at the Embassy, it said, "and guest."

Being new to the city, I didn't have anyone who fit the bill. But there was a young lady named Sachiko whom I'd seen several times at a restaurant close to my residence. She spoke English well, so, the next time I saw her there, I asked if she'd like to accompany me to meet the Queen. She readily agreed.

On the day of the party, I picked her up at the train station. She looked lovely in a fashionable spring outfit. While we managed to stand close to the Queen herself during the afternoon event, we were actually able to exchange a few pleasantries with the Prince during their walkabout.

Following the garden party a number of Canadians in attendance got together and went for dinner at a restaurant.

About a week later I received a phone call from one of the Canadians who'd joined us for dinner. He asked if I was watching television. I said I wasn't. He urged me to tune in to Channel 10 and a program called *Ginza Night Night*. It was a late-night show that was definitely for adult viewers. As the TV warmed up and the picture came into focus, I saw a young woman in an advanced stage of undress.

"Isn't that Sachiko?" he asked.

I had to admit, it certainly looked a lot like her.

It turns out that it *was* her. And I soon learned that she was one of Japan's leading stars of adult entertainment.

Thereafter, I became known as "that young diplomat who introduced the Queen of England to the Queen of the Night."

Robert Fairweather

West Vancouver, British Columbia

TALL ORDER

It was the first summer of the new millennium, and in Halifax there was a gathering of tall ships. Dozens of them arrived from around the globe for "Tall Ships 2000" as part of a spectacular race. The next port of call after Halifax was Amsterdam. Hundreds of thousands of people came to the city that summer to admire the white sails, the forest of masts, the crews, and the crowds. It was an awesome sight.

My wife, Michele, and I had become familiar with one of those beautiful ships—a fifty-seven-metre barquentine.

Michele is a sailmaker. She'd made a couple of the large square sails for the ship, and had accepted an invitation for both of us to be part of the crew on the Boston-to-Halifax leg of the race. We had the time of our lives. After the ship docked in Halifax we drove to our home near Lunenburg, got on board our own not-so-tall ship, and sailed back to the city. We picked up our daughter Amy so that she too could get a waterfront view of all the excitement. At the time, we had no idea just how exciting it was going to get.

Amy was between boyfriends then, and her part-time job was boring. Her life—she wouldn't mind me saying this—was in a rut. As we sailed around the busy harbour, she said wistfully, "Dad, there are times I wish I could just hop on board one of those ships and sail away."

A long moment of silence followed—then a totally crazy thought entered my mind:

Michele and I knew the captain. We knew the ship was seaworthy and safe. And we knew that if we could put Amy on that ship, the trip to Amsterdam would be something she'd remember for the rest of her life.

We figured there was no harm in asking. We sailed over to the pier where it was docked and asked to speak to the captain.

Frankly, we weren't expecting a yes, but that's what we got. Amy's eyes widened and our hearts pounded. What about her job? What about this? What about that? How would she get back to Canada? Amy said her employer would understand. We figured we could deal with the other things.

There was one other major obstacle: Amy would need a passport. She'd never travelled outside the country, and so didn't have one. The captain was adamant about this: "No passport, no Amsterdam."

It was Saturday afternoon. The ships were scheduled to sail Monday morning. It usually took weeks, if not months, to get a passport.

For those who haven't experienced it, let me tell you, being a crew member on a tall ship is special. The ship becomes your community. All members of the community must play a part in making everything work. It's magic, especially for a young person. And only a passport—or lack thereof—stood in the way of getting our daughter onto that ship and into the magic. We decided to go for it.

We knew Amy would need a professional photograph for the passport, so we docked our boat and ran through throngs of spectators to a well-known photography shop in the city. It was close to closing time, but we got the photo.

The next day, Sunday, a friend of ours who worked in the Lunenburg Post Office went in and got us an official application form. We filled it out, and the mayor of Lunenburg, who knew Amy, kindly signed the document and wished us luck. That night I barely slept as I rehearsed over and over what I was going to say to the people at the passport office.

Monday morning, July 24, 2000, dawned sunny in Halifax with white billowing clouds, a blue sky, and a light breeze. It was a perfect day for the huge Parade of Sail and the start of the race. CBC Television was live on the waterfront, with Peter Mansbridge broadcasting the sights and sounds across Canada. Halifax had rarely seen anything like it. The harbour was dotted with hundreds of boats, large and small. You couldn't get near the waterfront with a car.

I was at the passport office before eight o'clock with the application, references, photographs, telephone numbers, and every imaginable piece of identification. Amy, with a hastily packed duffle bag, walked down to the waterfront with Michele, hoping for the best. I was the first person at the wicket. I solemnly told the lady who waited on me that I was going to make a very unusual request. I told her the whole story—about how I came to be there before eight, and about how our daughter, as I spoke, was waiting on the wharf with my wife, praying that her dad could do the impossible—get a passport on the spot.

After I'd finished, she looked straight at me without saying a word for at least thirty seconds. Then she rolled her eyes as if to say, "So THIS is the kind of day I'm gonna have!"

Without a word, she took the documents and disappeared into a back office, where a conference of some sort resulted. Fifteen to twenty precious minutes went by before she came back out. I held my breath.

I'd give anything to know what was said in that back office, or who was called. All I know is that they agreed to do it. But I'd forgotten one vital detail: the guarantor who signed the passport application also had to sign the back of the photo-graph. This couldn't be done electronically, by fax, or by any other method. Our friend, the mayor, was in Lunenburg, normally about ninety minutes from downtown Halifax. By now it was after nine o'clock.

With the photograph in hand, I jumped in my car and headed back to Lunenburg. After all these years, I hope it's safe to confess that I was there in one hour flat.

Our good friend, the mayor, was waiting on his doorstep to sign the photograph. I thanked him again, did a U-turn, and headed back to Halifax, listening to CBC all the way. As I neared the city limits I heard that the ships were beginning to leave their berths to assemble for the beginning of the Parade of Sail.

Traffic was heavy. I parked my car at the first parking place I found and ran the rest of the way to the passport office. I found the woman I'd talked to earlier. I got the passport. I headed for the waterfront.

When I got there, the ship was gone and so was Amy. Michele said they'd had to leave.

The Parade of Sail required all the ships to circle Georges Island so that the media and spectators could get one last good look at them before they headed out to sea. We found a police security boat nearby that had docked for a few minutes. We tearfully asked if they would please take the passport out "to that big blue barquentine." They said they'd make sure it got to the ship.

Michele and I then walked to a lovely, if crowded, public viewing location not far from there. What a spectacular sight, as those ships—led by the *Bluenose II*—slowly made their way out of the harbour.

We shared our story with some people standing around us, and when Amy's ship came by, Michele and I were joined by at least a dozen other people, complete strangers to us, all shouting, "A-MEE, A-MEE, A-MEE!"

And out there, somewhere on that blue ship, was the daughter I had missed my chance to say goodbye to. Her life was about to change course—for the better. She had her passport.

Al Mosher

Lunenburg, Nova Scotia

AWAY IN A MANGER

I'm a veterinarian, so my family's used to my being paged, alerting me to animal emergencies. One such disruption, on Christmas Eve some years ago, was particularly memorable.

It was a perfect Christmas Eve. Snow was falling gently, and we were in church waiting for the service to begin. I sat back to listen to the music. Almost immediately, I got a call. A Mennonite farmer, who lived out of town, needed a veterinarian to help with a difficult calving. As quietly as possible I crawled out of the pew and headed into the night.

When a farmer calls about a calving, it generally means it's not going to be easy. The cow, I knew, must be in a bad way for me to be called out on Christmas Eve.

The weather had taken a turn for the worse. The snow was falling heavily now; the wind was angry. Christmas Eve on a backcountry road and the plows probably not at capacity—the drive was going to be difficult at best.

Before long I could hardly see the road; I had to roll down the window to get my bearings. What should have been a forty-five-minute drive turned into an hour and a half, and as time passed my chances of helping the cow deliver her calf were diminishing. I finally made it to the farm and turned up the lane. The farmer had no snow blower, indeed no vehicle, so the lane was almost impassable. I made it partway up with the four-wheel drive but then I got stuck.

When I finally reached the barn door I was puffing heavily.

The farmer greeted me quietly, but from his expression I could tell that he thought I was too late. We made our way to the pen. The cow was down, trying in vain to deliver her calf. I examined her: it was a breech birth. She was exhausted with the effort and turned her head away in defeat. But I'd come such a distance on this terrible night. I was determined to help her.

Half an hour later, stripped to the waist, covered in sweat from the exertion, I pulled out the baby calf. At first, nothing. He wouldn't breathe. But then his mother nudged him gently and his chest rose. The little fellow struggled to get up in the deep straw.

The farmer nodded to me in gratitude, and then asked if I'd like to dry off with some clean towels before we headed out into the night to dig out my truck. He hooked his lantern in the window. The barn door thudded softly behind him as he went to fetch the towels from the house. Exhausted, I sat down on a hay bale beside the stall and smiled at the calf's first attempts to nurse.

I'd been so preoccupied with the difficult labour that I hadn't noticed the absolute silence in the stable. All the other animals were staring in wonder at the newborn calf. He was staggering around the pen on wobbly legs, investigating his new surroundings.

And that's when I realized how intensely peaceful it was in that barn at that moment.

I sat there, in the golden glow of the lantern, feeling blessed to have been part of this birth, on a Christmas Eve, in a remote stable.

Marlene Leeper

Sechelt, British Columbia
(told to her by her friend, Dr. Reg Reed of Mitchell, Ontario)

STEPPING OUT

In 2002 my sister Clare, her husband, Terry, and their two teenage daughters came to visit us from the U.K. We arranged to rent an RV big enough for all of us, fully equipped with on-board kitchen and bathroom. The plan was to drive to Chicago, where we'd take in the sights and listen to some blues. So with my husband, Ben, and I sharing the driving, and Clare's family plus my one-year-old son and the dog safely in the back, we set off.

We crossed the border at Windsor, entered Detroit, and promptly got lost. By the time we found our way out to the I-94 we'd driven the thirty-foot RV through some of the less salubrious sights of the city, insults had been hurled about navigation and driving skills, tempers were frayed, and an unpleasant hush had descended.

We stopped at a rest area to switch drivers. I announced that I was going to use the washroom. I slammed the door and stormed off. When I came out a few minutes later I was greeted by the sight of the rear end of the RV hurtling down the slip road and back onto the interstate. I ran, screaming at the top of my voice, telling them to stop—to no avail.

They disappeared from sight, leaving me with no money and no cell phone.

At that moment, the driver of an eighteen-wheeler, about to leave the rest area, pulled up beside me and asked if I wanted to try to catch them. Any sane person would, and should, have said "No thanks," but the earlier insults and irritation over my map reading drove me to hurl caution to the wind. I hopped into the rig. The driver accelerated through the gears and the huge vehicle shuddered in pursuit. I sat back and immediately realized two things: I didn't know our RV's plate number and I couldn't remember my husband's cell phone number!

Back in the RV, my sister Clare had volunteered my brother-in-law Terry to drive. My husband was engrossed in directing Terry's driving when my niece began to wonder why I was taking so long in the RV's toilet. She got up and opened the door to the empty stall.

"Where's Margaret?" she cried.

At the same moment, a car drew up next to them and flashed a piece of paper against the window with the word "LADY" written on it and an arrow pointing back to the rest area. Pandemonium broke out. My brother-in-law, who was not at all confident driving the thing anyway, pulled over and practically jumped out of the seat. My husband took over.

Meanwhile, the trucker and I had spotted them up ahead. But just as we were about to catch up to them, they pulled off the highway and took the overpass. They headed back to the rest area just as we blew *under* the overpass in the eighteen-wheeler!

The truck driver pulled over as quickly as he could and got on his CB radio to ask truckers in the area for assistance.

Some of them asked my age, my marital status, and whether I was pretty, but others told him they'd look for the RV at the rest stop and, if they found it, would tell my family where they could find me.

Back at the rest stop everyone was frantically searching the washrooms. A torrential rain had begun to fall. My husband's mind was spiralling out of control; he was imagining terrifying possibilities of where his annoyed wife—on a mission to prove that her map-reading skills weren't as bad as he'd suggested—might turn up.

The American trucker and I, still waiting on the side of the highway, filled the time by chatting about Canada, and how he often listened to French-Canadian truckers chatting in French over the CB radio. After half an hour we decided that the RV wasn't coming to get me. He radioed his dispatcher. They said they'd send a state trooper to pick me up.

The state trooper eventually arrived and drove me back to the rest area, where I found my family. While I stood there forlornly, he told my teenage nieces never to do what I had done: never jump into a vehicle driven by someone you don't know!

Nevertheless, when we all got back into the RV, all the bad blood over our Detroit detour had vanished. The dog and my one-year-old son had slept through the entire affair. My brother-in-law never drove the RV again.

Margaret Walton-Roberts

Kitchener, Ontario

TREED

At the age of sixty-two, my father-in-law, who's had a lifelong affinity for impractical and highly entertaining adventures, decided to go tree planting. He'd always wondered what it was like. Three of his own kids, plus two kids-in-law, including me, had a combined total of nearly twenty summers of planting; together we'd planted close to two million trees, a small forest with our fingerprints all over it. Walter had heard more than his fair share of planting stories. He figured it was time to repay his ecological debts—forty years ago he'd worked as a logger. So when Paul, his youngest son, started recruiting for his own planting crew, Walter was first in line.

Paul and Walter left the flat acres of Kola, Manitoba, for the clear-cut patches of British Columbia's interior in early May. They joined a camp of eager rookies and seasoned vets whose mean age was roughly a third of Walter's. Walter won every one of them over right from the start, not just because he was the only guy in camp who looked like Walt Whitman, Karl Marx, or (let's not beat around the bush) Santa Claus, but because his true vocation in life is storytelling, and twenty-year-old tree planters love a good story as much as a classroom of kindergarteners.

Walter was the best of planters and Walter was the worst of planters. His technique was flawless—perfect depth, perfect spacing, and perfectly straight lines—but *perfect* tree planting requires a glacial pace, and that meant he wasn't making very much money. Add to that the gruelling intensity of the work, the solitude, the sub-zero nights, and the rainy days, plus missing Anne, his wife, and that grand adventure took a toll. His letters home were weary with discouragement.

At my wife's suggestion, I hopped the Greyhound and headed for Prince George to offer Walter some moral support and spend a few weeks planting some trees of my own. Walter gave me a big hug when we met at the camp. After he ate his supper, we sat under the tarp by his tent and he talked about how all of this was taking so much out of him. He'd decided he would stay until the end of the spring contract, another week or so, then go back to Kola. He felt that was respectable.

In my brief time there, I could see the important role Walter played, even if he was consistently out-planted by everyone else. He told great stories, of course, but he also listened—carefully—and had a deep well of empathy and encouragement for the others who struggled alongside him.

So, the day before the final week of Walter's tree-planting career, I wrote a letter to each of the crew bosses and asked if they could read it to their planters. I thought that, as a way to let Walter know how much everyone appreciated his presence, we could send him off with a big final-day tally. I invited everyone to chip in with whatever they could: a bundle of trees, a hundred, a thousand, or—why not?—a whole day's tally. I hoped that together we could come up with ten thousand trees for him—more than $1000. I knew everyone liked him, but still, I knew I was asking a lot.

Walter went back to his tent shortly after supper on his last day of work, but an eager group of us lingered as the day's tallies came in. Walter's final-day total began to grow. Paul's crew, the crew Walter was on, gave their whole day's tally, which put the count over ten thousand. Others came by to give the day's numbers to the crew bosses and threw a hundred or five hundred or more to Walter. I stayed up late, watching the tally grow.

I missed Walter's send-off the next morning. I had to catch an early-morning bus to Edmonton. But I heard later that the camp supervisor had called an end-of-contract camp meeting to talk about the next contract coming up and to send Walter on his way. He told the story of when he'd first met Walter, how he'd seemed like a pretty unlikely rookie, but that despite his numbers Walter was a really good planter and a vital member of the camp. Then he presented Walter with the survey map of the last block he'd planted, with his final tally inscribed on it with a Sharpie: twenty thousand trees, a $2000-plus send-off.

Tree planters are known for being a lot of things—scruffy, dirty, smelly, and occasionally bothersome seasonal visitors who stir up way too much trouble at the local bar. But I'd like to add one more item: generous, very generous.

Kurt Armstrong
Winnipeg, Manitoba

NO ORDINARY CAT

You never know the importance of your words and which of them might be taken seriously.

I learned this from a good buddy of mine—a cat named Boo Boo. Boo Boo was not an ordinary cat. He was an eighteen-year-old grey tabby with a regal bearing, Jack Nicholson eyes, and an enormous head. All of him was enormous. I have a tradition of huge cats, but Boo Boo was the champ. He weighed a hardy twenty pounds.

Sadly, he'd developed arthritis, which bowed his front legs and made him trundle when he walked. He also suffered seizures of increasing intensity, and eventually lost his meow altogether. He took to purring loudly when he wanted to communicate, or he'd open his mouth and make a rasping sound—a sort of pantomime meow. He was my buddy and my shadow. He followed me as I gardened.

In his last year the seizures increased, but he didn't seem to be suffering, despite all his maladies. He was always so affectionate that I couldn't bear to put him down. I kept waiting for a sign that enough was enough.

His last seizure was in August out on our deck.

After his jerking stopped, I knelt to comfort him, and while I petted him I said, "You've got to help me out here, buddy; I don't know what to do about you."

After a few minutes he seemed fine. He shook himself off and went to drink out of the plant water. I went upstairs and hopped into the shower. While I was in the bathroom I heard a truck, but paid it no attention. My twenty-five-year-old son, Josh, had come racing home to gather some tools from our shop. In his haste he jumped out of the truck, left the motor running, and bolted into the shop. Tools in hand, he leaped back into the truck, put it in gear, and took off. Immediately, he hit something.

All I heard was "Oh my god. No!"

Boo Boo had lain down in front of the rear wheel on the passenger side of Josh's truck. Josh hadn't seen him. Josh took off his T-shirt, wrapped it around Boo Boo, and carried the injured animal to the cab of his truck. He raced to the vet with the cat in his lap.

When Josh got to the clinic he gently gathered Boo Boo in his arms and rushed in shirtless, his chest scratched and bleeding. Through tears he said to the receptionist, "You've got to save him, I ran over him."

But it was too late. Boo Boo was dead.

The news crushed Josh. The entire staff gathered around him and the dead cat. They were so touched to see this young man weeping that they became tearful, too.

Josh brought the cat home to me wrapped in his bloody T-shirt. Boo Boo looked peaceful and was still warm to the touch. We laid him on the grass on the front lawn, both of us petting him and crying. I told Josh the whole story about

Boo Boo's last seizure and how I'd asked him to help me know what to do with him.

"Josh," I said through my tears, "I'm convinced that he *did* help me out by lying under your truck."

We cried together and eulogized Boo Boo until my husband came home. That night we buried our buddy. Josh made a stout wooden cross that I can still see from my front window.

I miss him of course. But to this day I maintain that it wasn't an accident.

Susan Grout

Friday Harbor, Washington

A CURRENT
OF KINDNESS

In 2005, my friend Drew Osborne and I embarked on a five-month, six-thousand-kilometre canoe trip.

The expedition began on the snowy banks of the North Saskatchewan River in late April and ended on a glorious fall day on the St. Lawrence River in Montreal. It was an experience of a lifetime shared between two friends.

Conquering the grand wilderness of Canada in a canoe is both unimaginably challenging and stunningly beautiful. We paddled up and down rivers, over waves, rocks, and sandbars, and across some of the world's largest lakes. We saw it all.

On our seventieth day we began our first upstream battle, against the current on the Winnipeg River. Paddling against the record flood proved to be more emotionally draining than it was physically (as if surviving the Manitoba bug season wasn't enough).

It took an entire day to cover what we normally covered in an hour. After three long days of this, the force against us began to take its toll. Evening drew near and we struggled to find a place to camp amidst the cottages on the banks of the river, our exhaustion turning to frustration. As our weary, bug-bitten arms dipped our paddles into the river, we began to wonder if it was possible to continue.

Up in the distance we saw a man standing on his dock as if awaiting our arrival. When we were within earshot he called out to us. He asked where we were going.

We replied, "Montreal!"

"I doubt you'll make it to Montreal tonight," he laughed. "How about you call it a day and stay with us?"

It was perfect.

Al and his wife, Lynn, invited us into their beautiful cottage for the evening. When Lynn took one look at our bloody, swollen bug bites, our dirty clothes, and our messy hair, she insisted we each take a bath. It was our first bath in over seventy days, long overdue and simply magnificent.

After we'd each bathed and it was possible to stand within ten feet of us, Lynn approached us holding a telephone.

"Call your mothers," she said.

She said they'd want to know we were safe and doing well. She was right. We had an amazing dinner, lovely conversation, and, under fresh sheets, we fell into deep sleeps. As I drifted off, I remember wondering what I'd done to deserve the generosity of these total strangers.

In the morning we had another wonderful meal and then began our preparations to continue. Lynn had prepared fresh-baked goods for us to take on the journey.

As we paddled away we were beaming. Our strokes were powerful and strong. I don't think we even noticed that the river was flowing against us. At the time I felt so lucky to have met these inspiring people. As we continued, we found that this was just the first example of the incredible generosity of strangers. Every time we thought we couldn't go any farther it seemed there was someone else waiting with a warm meal and a fire.

I learned a lot of things on this trip. Many things I will never be able to put into words.

One thing that continues to resonate with me is how inspiring it was to meet such giving people. They opened my eyes and my heart to the simple beauty of generosity. As I reflect on this trip years later, I feel a profound gratitude for this gift.

Clare Cayley
Vancouver, British Columbia

U.S. POSTAGE

AMOUNT

.03

PAID

METER 01312

YEAR NINE

MAC AND CHEESE

I don't know about you, but when I think of comfort food—the kind that can be slathered like sunscreen over wounded egos, homesickness, and disappointment, the sort that evokes home and hearth and safety—there's only one food I think of, and that's macaroni and cheese. Not the stuff in the box, the real thing.

My mother's macaroni and cheese was plain—elbow noodles and a medium cheese sauce mixed together, topped with buttered bread crumbs and baked in the oven till golden and bubbling. It was one of my favourite meals—until the summer when, as a university student, I worked at a lodge on Gabriola Island, where Bertie Turner introduced me to a whole new kind of macaroni and cheese.

Every Wednesday, guests were given a picnic lunch and encouraged to go exploring. While they set off, the staff would congregate in the huge log lounge and do a thorough cleaning, including polishing the hardwood floors. At lunchtime we'd troop into the kitchen to sit around the long rustic table, laughing and joking as if we were a large, boisterous European family. Lunch was always the same on Wednesdays: a crisp green salad and Bertie's wonderful macaroni and cheese. She baked it in a wide shallow pan and cut it into squares for serving. The bottom layer was caramelized onions, and then the quiche-like, cheesy middle, topped with thinly sliced beefsteak tomatoes and sprinkled with buttery crumbs. From that summer on, I was convinced that my mother didn't know anything about macaroni and cheese. Bertie's was the best in the world.

As an adult, I spent years, without success, trying to reproduce Bertie's macaroni and cheese. I think I felt that if I could match its flavour and texture, I'd feel as happy and carefree as I did that long-ago summer. Driven by a desire to produce an even better version, the ultimate comfort meal, I'd often include extra ingredients. But while they might have been tasty and even nutritious, I never achieved the effect I was hoping for.

And then one autumn evening, when the smoke from the chimneys was rising straight up into the crisp still air, the sky brightened and an enormous orange moon pushed its way above the trees and hung heavy and ripe in front of me. And I was transported to another autumn evening. The full moon rising above the treetops and me, riding on my father's shoulders, so high that I felt I could reach out and touch it. Reach out and touch the moon and the spiky treetops and the little frost sparkles that seemed to be falling through the air.

It was the only time I rode on my father's shoulders. He was a distant man, never playful or affectionate like my friends' fathers. Whenever he looked at me, I saw disapproval rather than love in his eyes. It felt as if he was always correcting me. But that evening I was coming home from the hospital. I'd had a routine operation that had gone wrong, and I'd had to stay longer than planned. All the way home he kept his big callused hand over mine, as if he was making sure I was safe. It felt strange, but in a nice way. When we got out of the car I was amazed when he hoisted me onto his shoulders. I was so high I felt as if I were flying. I spread my arms wide. I felt as wild as the owls I'd seen swooping out of the forest. Head back, I gazed up at the stars before turning to see the moon's enormous orange face smiling back at me. Down the long path to the house my father carried me, without a word, and I loved him more with every step. I could feel him smiling in the dark and I knew that he loved me too.

When we sat down at the table, my mother took a dish of macaroni and cheese out of the oven, all golden and crispy on top with creamy sauce bubbling through it here and there. I savoured every bite, scraping my fork over my plate to capture every crumb, every bit of creamy sauce, all the while aware of the new closeness of my father.

As the memory of that long-ago night faded, I turned and went into my house to prepare macaroni and cheese the way my mother used to make it. Nothing fancy: just elbow macaroni and a medium cheese sauce with buttered crumbs on top.

"Macaroni and cheese," said my husband as I set it on the table. "What kind is it?"

"The good kind," I said, smiling through the window at the moon.

Vicki Drybrough
Port Alberni, British Columbia

A MODEL BOYHOOD

There are four brothers in my family, and we all grew up building, and trying to fly, balsa-wood model aircraft.

My early efforts, as I remember them, were mostly glue and fingerprints. Rough, heavy, and warped, they neither "climbed" nor "soared." My brothers and I had fun building them and playing with them, but I remember clearly the moment when my lifelong fascination with flight really took hold.

My dad was reluctant to make large financial investments in a continual supply of fragile models, but on one rare trek to the hobby shop, while I puzzled over which tiny balsa-and-tissue model I would savage this time, my dad's attention was absorbed by a kit on the higher shelves.

"What do you think of this?" he asked. I wasn't impressed, actually. It was a simple-profile, delta catapult-launch glider. A kind of scaled-up version of the five-cent glider from the candy store. I didn't want it because it looked simplistic. I thought I was more advanced.

My dad thought I should try it. He pointed out that the model required a lot of work: the parts were printed, not die cut. It would require patience and sanding to make the wings into airfoils. More importantly, it could be fitted with a Jetex rocket engine. He made me a deal: if I did a good job with the glider, and got it flying, we'd get the Jetex engine and fly it under power.

Talk about a kid consumed. I thought of nothing else. I spent that summer carving the fuselage to specifications, sanding the wings to perfection, and aligning all the surfaces with precision. Laser beams cannot carve a straighter line than an eight-year-old's hand and eyes, given the proper motivation. I studied the set-up and trimming instructions meticulously. I carried out flight testing in scientifically planned stages, finally culminating in a glorious seventeen-second maiden voyage.

True to the deal, my dad and I picked up the Jetex engine. There was no need to study the instructions. Somehow, in those pre-internet years, my eight-year-old brain managed to master the physics of rocket propulsion and had accumulated an intimate knowledge of the engineering and safe operation of all the models in the Jetex line. After some simple heat-proofing modifications, I attached the engine. My newly rocket-powered glider was ready for testing.

For those who aren't familiar with the Jetex engine, allow me a moment to explain the basics. It's a small tin cylinder with a hole in one end for thrust gases to escape. You insert fuel tablets that look like compressed clay, coil a wick against the fuel pellets, and lead it out through the exhaust pinhole. The idea is to cut the length of fuse to equal the delay time required to a) light the fuse, b) catapult-launch the aircraft, and c) allow the aircraft to reach the apex of rubber-powered flight. If everything goes right, your rocket thrust engages at just the right time and up you go.

Jetex fuel comes in a package with fuel tablets, special screens, gaskets for six flights, and precisely enough of the incredibly fragile igniter wick for two flights. The problem is further compounded by the fact that the igniter works only once every eighteen tries, and the flame is readily extinguished upon reaching the exhaust hole. The first day, I think I actually had about eighteen or twenty "failures to ignite," two ground burns (launched, landed, then ignited), and one burn where I held on to the plane until it was burning, then chucked it just as it was running down. Dad and I got to the hobby store just as they were closing, to get more wick.

The next morning I was ready and anxious to try again. Waiting for full daylight was not a big priority. I remember the dew on the grass. I guess the sky was a beautiful colour, and lazy morning clouds were glowing in the rising light. I guess I was surrounded by the quiet that accompanies the start of a summer day. I don't remember. All I was concerned about was whether the dew would get that darned wick wet and cause me problems.

I had prepared the night before, winding a precision coil of igniter fuse on a lightly sanded fuel pellet, installing the cover carefully so the fuse was perfectly sized and placed. The frustration and haste of the day before had been replaced with quiet certainty. My muscle memory was prepared for the much-practised routine. Dad had loaned me his Zippo, which proved more reliable than the paper matches I'd struggled with in the breeze. I prepared myself—light the fuse, wait for a steady burn, stand, string the catapult on the hook, stretch, wait … wait. A hot spark landed on my forearm. I held my breath waiting for the wick to sputter through the little exhaust hole. When it reached the hole there were about four seconds till it would ignite, about six seconds to begin burning. Wait …

You know it right away when it happens. Flight, I mean. A clever engineer once won a paper airplane distance competition by wrapping a rock with paper and throwing it. But that was a loophole in the rules, not flight. This was really something new to me.

The little dart flew beautifully, arcing up straight and true in the still air as it had done so many times before, but this time, just as the flight began to level out, the little jet engine sputtered and puffed, a thin stream appeared, and the plane began to rise again, coaxing lift from the meagre thrust of the jet. It soared to three times the height it had ever gone. I began to wonder if it would get away!

I began my leggy pursuit, stumbling along as I struggled to keep my bird in view. Looking back momentarily, I saw my dad watching from the steps by our old house.

Peter Goddard

Burlington, Ontario

AFTER THE WAR

My most memorable Remembrance Day did not occur in November, but rather in May 1964.

Barely out of my teens, I was in first year at the University of Toronto. With my strong background in Army Cadets I'd landed a summer job with the Canadian military. I would be trained during the next few summers to become an army officer.

First there were the tedious, but necessary, medical tests at Sunnybrook Medical Centre. Back then, Sunnybrook was totally devoted to treating active military personnel and injured war veterans, many of whom lived there permanently in long-term care.

I marched onto the hospital grounds in my stiff new uniform and my squeaky new boots, my medical file under my arm. I was headed for X-rays.

I saw the wheelchair first. It was parked on a gravel path beside a beautiful flowerbed.

As I got closer, I saw a blue plaid blanket draped across the man's lap. There were no feet visible, only the outline of two stumps. As I kept walking I saw that the man's right arm was amputated.

When I got close enough to make eye contact, I was shaken by what my youthful eyes saw. This man's face was greatly disfigured. It was red. It looked burned. His left eye was almost totally shut. A lit cigarette dangled awkwardly from the three fingers that remained of his left hand. It was hard for me to look at him. But I knew I'd have to greet him in passing.

When I mumbled "Good morning," the man contorted his pained face into a smile.

"Good morning, sir," he said.

The man must have noticed my single-rank pip with the strip of white cloth, indicating my lowly Officer Cadet status. What right did I have to be called "sir" by this veteran soldier, who was probably older than my grandfather?

As the man continued to speak, I found it increasingly difficult to listen to him.

"If you don't mind me saying so, sir," he said, "just look at how wonderful a spring day we're blessed with today! Does it not make you feel wonderful just to be alive?"

A lump formed in my throat. I felt embarrassed by the tears that were creeping into my eyes. How could this man find anything to be joyful or glad about?

My military pride would not allow me to linger any longer.

"It *is* a beautiful day," I uttered, affecting a husky, masculine tone. "But you'll have to excuse me, I'm almost late for my next appointment."

"Oh, of course, sir," he replied. "I'm sorry for delaying you."

Then he raised his three-fingered hand in a respectful salute.

"Not at all," I replied flatly. I returned his salute and marched off as the first tear escaped the corner of my eye.

The nurse inside told me that the man's name was Charlie.

She told me he'd been injured in a gas and artillery attack in France. He'd been confined to the wheelchair and hospital for close to fifty years.

It has been more than four decades since my one brief encounter with Charlie, and I think of him often. When I do, I'm filled with a sense of awe and respect for the indomitable quality of the human spirit.

Alan Nanders

Kitchener, Ontario

CHRISTMAS EVE

It was Christmas Eve on the Children's Ward. The few lights on the small tree in the centre of the room reflected softly on the rows of white metal cribs and tiny white beds that lined both sides of the ward.

Although it was only seven-thirty in the evening, all the parents had left and the children had been settled for the night. Each had received the necessary bedtime treatments and medications. It was time to sleep. But only the very young and the very ill had done so. All the other children sat quietly and despondently in their beds, their eyes wide open.

Everyone—staff as well as children—longed to be home with families and friends on this special night. Each child's face showed the same sombre anxiety: Would Santa know they weren't at home in their own beds and, if he did, would he be able to find them in the frightening maze of corridors and connecting doors of the hospital?

There had been a Santa in visiting the ward that afternoon. He wore a red suit and had a long white beard. He jingled his bells constantly and called out frequently in a loud voice, "Ho, ho, ho!" He left each of them a small gift. But he had left no joy.

As the lights in the big ward were dimmed, we became aware of a figure standing in the doorway—a member of the Royal Canadian Mounted Police decked out in full dress uniform.

A chorus of small gasps filled the room. To the staff, our visitor represented the law, but to the children, he was a symbol of mystery and adventure.

He stood there for several minutes in his Stetson hat, scarlet tunic, breeches, and shining brown leather boots. He didn't say a word.

Then he walked quickly to the first small bed, pulled up the nearest chair, and began an earnest and private conversation with its young occupant. We couldn't hear what he was saying, and he obviously didn't intend us to hear. His words were only for the child. He stayed for a few minutes and then moved quietly to the next bed.

He stood silently by the crib of a very ill baby, holding the small hand in his for several minutes and then leaning over to place a gentle kiss on the forehead of the sleeping child. His conversations varied with each little person. Some were sombre and soft, some were private whispers, others became animated and jolly. He stayed the same length of time with each, not missing a bed.

Our visitor left as silently as he'd come. There were no "Ho, ho, hos," no calls of "Merry Christmas," and no parcels, but each child had received a priceless gift—a few minutes of his undivided attention, a few minutes of being special.

Two hours later, when the evening supervisor made her routine rounds, I mentioned the visitor and she said, "Oh, I'm sorry, I should have told you. He comes every Christmas to visit the children. He lost his own son on this ward several years ago. It was at this time of year. Every year since, he's made a visit in his memory."

Marion McNaught
(submitted by her daughter Karen Careless of Gibsons, British Columbia)

RIDING THE RUNNERS

I met a man on a bus one snowy day. He told me a wonderful story. As we sat looking out the window, he told me how glittery snow always took him back to the Christmas he turned nine.

His name was André. He was born in 1946, the tenth of fourteen children on a Quebec farm. He was less than a year younger than his brother and best friend, Guy. He and Guy did everything together. They shared chores, clothes, and a bed.

They also shared a dream.

The family lived on a farm at the end of a country road that was never plowed. When the snow came each winter, the only mode of transportation, other than walking, was by horse and sleigh. Every Christmas there was a candlelight service at the local church. So if the family was going, they could only go by sleigh.

The sleigh didn't have enough seats for all the family. For the candlelight service, the youngest children would ride on the floor of the sleigh, snuggled close to the warm bricks that were placed under everyone's feet and covered with bearskin rugs. The oldest two boys took turns riding up front with their dad, helping with the team. Everyone else crowded onto the seats with their mother. Everyone except two boys. Every Christmas two boys were chosen to ride on the runners of the sleigh, holding on to the rope their father had tied back there.

Being chosen to ride on the runners was a rite of passage. There were rules. You had to be eight or older, and you had to be able to reach the rope comfortably.

André was a small child. So he continued to ride in the sleigh for two Christmases while Guy rode the runners. As the Christmas after his ninth birthday approached, he and Guy had anxious conversations about whether this would be the year they'd get to ride the runners together.

Christmas Eve dinner dragged that year as they awaited their father's customary post-dinner seating plan announcement. When he finally made the announcement, they couldn't believe it: their wish had come true. They would be riding the runners together!

It seemed to take forever for their father and brothers to get the team ready and even longer for the bricks and bearskin rugs to warm by the wood stove. Finally the grand moment arrived.

André told me the memory of that night still brings him joy. There was a full moon, he said, and the new snow on the trees and fields glistened like diamonds. The bells on the horses' harnesses jingled with every step. Sitting beside me on that bus, André chuckled at the memory of his mother's silhouette appearing over the back of the sleigh. *"Ça va bien?"* she asked them again and again.

Guy and André rode the runners for the next two Christmases, until Guy was promoted to the driver's seat and André became big brother to the next boy in line.

Every year at this time, I think of my bus ride with André, and of the sleigh ride he took so many years ago: those two little boys, their eyes twinkling like diamonds under the full moon. Their giggles echoing in my heart all these years later.

It's his story, but as the years pass, his memory of that sleigh ride has slowly become one of my favourite Christmas memories, although it doesn't belong to me at all.

Charlotte Fraser

Bedford, Nova Scotia

LOVE STORY

This story needs a better ending—a Valentine's Day ending.

It starts at one of the handful of repertory movie houses that survive in Toronto. I could go on about how much I love rep theatres—the just-right scale of them, neither "colossus" nor "overgrown living room"; the lack of video-arcade hype and outlandish pricing—but that's not why I'm writing.

It was my birthday. I'd gone to see a movie with a girlfriend.

I'm single, widowed far too young and for far too long. At first I tried to change that story. I dated men a computer found for me—good matches on paper, but no soul fit. I believe in soul fit. I believe love finds you. Maybe that's why I was at this particular movie on my birthday. It was a love story. I wanted to keep *believing*.

A man sat across the aisle from me. He was pleasant looking; he had a newspaper folded thin under one arm. He ate his big bag of popcorn with ungainly enthusiasm. He smiled easily.

The theatre grew dark and I was engrossed. I won't describe how susceptible I am to movies. It's embarrassing.

But as the closing titles rolled, I thought again of the man across the aisle. Why couldn't I meet someone like him?

Suddenly I remembered the old story about the man at sea. Nearly drowning, he refuses three offers of help, saying that God will save him—that he's waiting for God—and then … he drowns. When he gets to heaven, he asks St. Peter why God didn't save him and St. Peter says, "We sent you a rowboat, a life raft, and a submarine. What more did you expect?"

What more did *I* expect? He was sitting a few feet away. It was my birthday. You're supposed to take chances on your birthday.

So, for the first time in four decades, I decided to take a chance. I stood in the aisle behind him and tried to speak. This is where my near decade of singleness collided with a case of indescribable nerves. He looked up and smiled in such a way as to freeze me into immobility. Then he stood and left the theatre. I compelled my limbs to move.

A crowded movie lobby doesn't do anything to ease the nerves. He was through the door. He stood outside in the pool of light spilling out onto the sidewalk, putting on his coat. "Excuse me," I blurted.

Somehow, I explained. "I don't usually do this. It's my birthday. So I'm just going to ask you if, um, by any chance you're single?"

"As a matter of fact, I am." He said it sheepishly, looking down and then up with a smile, and I was … well, I was thrilled. We chatted, he wished me a happy birthday, and then he offered to take me for a drink.

In a fit of misguided loyalty I told him I couldn't. I'd come with a friend.

"I can't ditch her—it wouldn't be right—but I'd really like to do that sometime. Can I give you my number?" I scrawled my number on his newspaper. He walked with me to the corner where I saw my friend. I floated across the street to meet her.

I beamed a look at her that said, "I did it!"

As I explained what happened, I could see it vividly—the number I wrote on that paper. It was *my* number all right—when I was twelve.

My *old* brain had lurched into action and I'd written my childhood telephone number on that paper.

I ran—no, I *pelted*—back to find him.

He was gone.

The worst part isn't losing track of that man—the worst part is the thought that he might be as good a guy as he seemed. He might pick up the phone and get the operator's voice that's now at the end of that number, and he might think it was a cruel trick. But it was just the opposite. It was a leap of faith.

I put a note on the theatre's website and left a card at the ticket booth addressed to Nick. Nick, that's all I know, no number, no address, just a face, a name, and faith.

Jill Kelsall
Toronto, Ontario

A REUNION

My sister and I were born in Somerset, England, and we enjoyed a carefree childhood until the Second World War broke out. That was when our mother decided we'd be better off living in America—families in the United States were offering safe haven for English children for the duration of the war. She figured we'd be gone a year at the most. I was seven years old. My sister was a few years older.

A couple of months later we boarded an ocean liner, along with maybe three hundred other evacuated children. We were leaving all we knew and loved behind, and looking ahead to a strange new world. My sister and I were sent to live with a family in Newton, Massachusetts. They cared for and looked after us for the next six years. We became part of their family. As time went on it became hard for me to believe that one day I would return to a country I couldn't remember, and to a mother who would be a stranger to me.

I was thirteen when the war came to an end. Suddenly it was time for me to go back to England. This time I'd be travelling alone, as my sister was in college and wouldn't be returning for a few more months. Shortly before I left, my mother sent me a small parcel. I opened it and found a triangular piece of material; it was navy blue and had a pattern of small white polka dots. I had no idea why she'd sent it until I read the note. The note said that the piece of material had originally been a square, and that my mother had cut the square into two triangles. When she met the boat at Southampton, she wrote, she'd be wearing her half of the square as a headscarf. She'd like me to wear the other half. That way we would recognize each other when the boat docked.

My mother was obviously as nervous about our meeting as I was. She'd realized that I was no longer the blond seven-year-old she had said goodbye to. There was no email or Skype or any of the other technologies we can use today when people are apart.

I sailed home on the *Queen Mary*. It had been used as a troop ship during the war, and this was its first voyage home as a passenger liner. I was put in the care of a young couple who'd just been married. As luck would have it, they were more interested in each other than in me—which meant that for the five-day crossing I had the freedom to wander wherever I wanted.

The days passed happily enough. There was wonderful food and lots of decks to explore. In the evenings I'd go to the ship's lounge and watch movies. I stayed up way past my official bedtime. Finally, however, the boat docked in Southampton. Finally the moment of truth.

I decided I wouldn't wear the headscarf. I wanted to see my mother before she saw me.

So, bareheaded, I went on deck and looked over the railing. I searched for her among the throng of excited parents on the dock. It took only a couple of minutes for me to spot her in the crowd. She was wearing the scarf. I started waving and calling to her, forgetting I had no scarf on my head. She was waving to someone farther down the deck. It didn't matter. She was my mother and all the love and longing I had suppressed for six years came flooding to the surface. I couldn't wait to disembark and run to her.

I watched her realize her mistake, and then I watched her searching through the throng of young children. She finally saw me for who I was—a teenager with a big wide grin, slightly darker hair, and a wave that could only be meant for her.

A few weeks later, after I was safely settled at home, she told me what it was like for *her* when the *Queen Mary* docked and she saw all the children waving and calling out. She told me she'd completely forgotten she was looking for a teenage girl wearing a navy blue headscarf. She told me that, in her joy and relief, she'd been waving to a little bareheaded blond girl who must have been about seven or eight years old. In that moment the six long years of waiting had melted away; her little one had been safely and miraculously returned to her.

We put the scarves away after that. They hadn't been needed then, nor were they ever needed again.

Sheila Hutton

Fredericton, New Brunswick

ADRIFT IN
PEACE RIVER

About five or six years ago, I moved from Yellowknife to Fort Smith, Northwest Territories. Once I'd settled in my new home, I decided it was time for a road trip to visit friends in Calgary.

I left Fort Smith on a Monday morning. After six hours on the road I decided to make a stop to wash the car and get gas in High Level, Alberta. Leaving the car wash, I pulled back onto the highway and soon went into the kind of trance that I fall into on these northern roads. The landscape in this part of the world is hard to describe. While hardly stunning or full of landmarks, it's still pretty and varied. But at the same time, every kilometre looks the same as the one before.

So deep into my trance was I that I didn't see the sign for the OSB plant, which for some reason has always been an important landmark for me. I also missed the sign telling me how far Peace River was. Not long after I'd noticed my fogginess, I crossed a bridge that I didn't recognize. It had been a couple of years since I'd been out that way, and I thought, How quickly we forget these things. Anyway, there sure were a whole lot more oil and gas developments than there'd been the last time I drove the route. I was starting to get drowsy, so about a hundred kilometres out of High Level I pulled over for a ten-minute nap. I couldn't get far off the side of the road and began to worry that traffic—trucks in particular—might wake me when they passed. To my surprise I slept soundly for those few minutes—the traffic, I thought to myself, was unusually light.

It wasn't until I was another forty kilometres down the road when it hit me like a logging truck on a blind curve. I managed to put all the pieces together—something you probably did quite some time ago. I was closing in on Rainbow Lake, which was the end of a different road from the one I should have been on. A quick check of the map showed me that I'd driven 140 kilometres *west* when I should have been heading *south*.

There was no road connecting Rainbow Lake with anywhere else other than back to High Level.

I had no choice but to retrace my route.

By evening I was exhausted. I decided to call it quits and stop for the night in Peace River.

Tuesday morning I left my Peace River hotel room to put my bags in my car before grabbing breakfast. Walking out the side door that I'd come in through from the parking lot the previous evening, I was a little stunned to find my car had disappeared. I always half expect my polar bear licence plate to be half-inched when I'm in Alberta, but not my whole car! I quickly realized, though, that I'd parked in a no-parking zone, so it was with some relief that I figured I'd probably been towed. The front desk didn't know anything about that. So I borrowed a phone book and called the one towing company in it. They told me they knew nothing about my car. They did say, however, that they weren't allowed to tow a car just because it was illegally parked. If they were going to tow a car they had to be asked by the RCMP.

I hitched a ride to the cop shop and asked whether they knew anything about my car. The extremely helpful desk agent called everyone she could, and half an hour later announced that she didn't have any good news. My car *had* been stolen!

I filled out the appropriate forms, and was introduced to the constable who'd be handling my case. I got the impression that any confidence he had came from his uniform and the gun hanging from his belt rather than from within himself, especially when he wrote down my licence number incorrectly. I was at the station for ninety minutes. While there, I lost any faith that my car would be found.

As I left, I wondered what on earth I should do. Obviously someone was trying to tell me that I wasn't supposed to be going to Calgary. I got that, but how was I going to get home? As far as I knew there was no airport in Peace River, and who would drive ten hours from Fort Smith to pick me up? It was no use calling any of my friends in Yellowknife. The ferry wasn't in yet so they were completely cut off. I hadn't been planning on buying another car, but perhaps that was my best option.

Looking back on this string of calamities, I'm proud to say that I didn't become even slightly upset. I accepted my fate. I was in a bit of a predicament. But I was most miffed about the prescription glasses that were missing along with my car.

I got a cab to take me back to the hotel. The driver insisted on giving me his card, and said, "I hope that next time I'll get to pick you up from somewhere else!" I think he thought I'd been in the drunk tank overnight. I told him I was a cop. He put on his seatbelt and shut up.

On the journey, a thought that I couldn't shake had begun to bug me.

Climbing out of the cab, I walked around to the side of the hotel where the parking lot was, and there, exactly where I'd left it the previous night, was my car. That morning I'd lost my bearings and exited on the wrong side of the building into an identical parking lot.

I went back to my room to call the cop I'd dealt with and ask him to take my car off the "wanted" list. You can't imagine how humble I felt.

Next, I went to check out.

"Did you find your car?" asked the girl at the front desk.

"Oh yes," I said. "Thanks. That's all taken care of." And I hurriedly departed.

All thoughts of Calgary abandoned, I got in my car and headed for home.

Ben Avern

Victoria, British Columbia

POSTMARKED

My eighty-eight-year-old mom phoned the other night. She phoned to tell me that the mailbox at the corner of her street had disappeared. This may not sound like disturbing news to you, but *I* found it disturbing.

I knew right away which mailbox she meant: the one on the hydro pole at the corner of Broadway and Torrington in Ottawa's Glebe neighbourhood. It had been there for over seventy-five years. It's a neighbourhood landmark. As children we were told, "Don't go past the mailbox." Mrs. Lennox, our elderly next-door neighbour at the time, would give us a chocolate bar to run to the box and mail her letters. Coming home late as teenagers, so as not to have car noise in front of the house, the drop point was, you guessed it, the mailbox. And after Dad's hip operation last year, when he could walk to the mailbox and back, we knew he was going to be just fine.

Over the years, hundreds of thousands of letters, Christmas cards, birthday greetings, and sympathy notes have been posted there and sent all over the world—feelings and sentiments, wishes and thoughts.

I'm writing this letter on the ferry to Vancouver. Tomorrow

I'm flying to Ottawa for two weeks with my parents. Now, when I send my postcards home to B.C., I'll no longer be able to take the familiar walk to the corner to post them. Instead I'll have to get in the car, drive ten or twelve blocks to the nearest post office, and hope there's a parking spot. It's not the same.

That stoic little red soldier has been at its post for hundreds of seasons, weathering sun and rain, snow and ice. Through World War II, and over ten prime ministers. Its welcoming slot has accepted generations of paid bills, life stories, and shared secrets.

Canada Post tells me that a mailbox needs fifty letters a day to remain viable. Our corner mailbox no longer met this criteria and it had to go. I've suggested they put it back, sealed up, as a piece of neighbourhood history, as an artifact. I have not received a response.

I'm very aware that things are changing rapidly all around me. I'm told that I should accept these changes and adapt. Every once in a while, though, one of these changes upsets a balance in my heart, or a memory, and there's an impulse to reject the "new" way. This is one of those times. I believe that the culture and history of a neighbourhood deserve to be protected. The mailbox at the corner was an eloquent testament to times gone by.

Mary Cook
Duncan, British Columbia

THE OLD BUICK

My parents are two of the most interesting people I will ever meet. They met, fell in love (my father choked out a proposal), and they were married. September 1, 1985. Four years later they had my older sister, then two years after that they had me. I remember a lot from my early years, but the things that stick with me the most are our family vacations.

The trips themselves were memorable, but what was most memorable was the car we travelled in. A gold four-door 1979 Buick Electra—Limited Edition. It was bought new out of a catalogue by my dad's dad. My sister and I called it the Loser Cruiser. At almost nineteen feet long, we could go for weeks with all our stuff packed in there, and we often did.

I remember my father in the driver's seat, constantly streaming trivia about the buildings we were whooshing past. When he paused to breathe, my mother would lower the visor and flip open the mirror to look at my sister and me. If we looked comatose she would ask loudly, "Girls, are you soaking up the culture?"

As I watched the fields blur past my window, she would

proclaim, "Yellow flowers!" to which we were expected to respond promptly, "Canola!"

Yellow flowers for canola, blue for flax, purple for alfalfa, and pink for clover.

Although the destinations always had a purpose, at least half the fun was the journey.

The older we got, the more unreliable the Buick became. Each road trip was a gamble. The week before we'd leave, Dad would take me to junkyards where he'd point out similar models and rifle through their engines or dashboards in search of whatever part had just given up. He'd spend the night before we left repairing the Buick, which was parked on the dark street out in front of the house, packed and ready to go, a work light hooked onto the raised hood.

Since those days, my sister and I have grown up and moved to different areas of the West Coast. The Buick still sits outside my parents' house, its days coming to an end. It's harder and harder to maintain. The parts we need to fix it up have become more and more scarce. It's sad to see it sitting there, but I know it's had a long, fulfilling life: packed with adventure and a loving family that tried their best to keep it running as long as they could.

A few days before I left home, I went and sat in the Buick for what I think may have been the last time. I sat in the back, behind the driver's seat, *my* seat on all those road trips. I couldn't bring myself to sit in the front because those seats didn't belong to me: they belonged to my parents. I closed the door and shut my eyes, remembering. The car still smelled the same—musty and comforting—and the seat felt the same, too. I visualized the tower of pillows that I used to stack between my sister and me in case she tried to look at me. I felt the wind tangle my hair as we drove with all four windows down because the air conditioner had died again.

I thought of the trips, yes, but I also thought of everything that had led me to that moment and place. In just days I'd be moving far away—a thousand kilometres. Somehow, it didn't seem too scary to be going so far. My father's trivia and my mother's comments made even a thousand kilometres feel like it was just around the block. Whether they knew it or not, when they took me on those trips they were preparing me for the world outside our neighbourhood. They were preparing me for the day when I'd have to leave it and explore on my own. Everything they did back then was for me; now it's my turn. Everything I do is for them. Every favour I do for a friend, every test I study hard for, every extra mile I go to make someone feel valued—I do for my parents.

And though I may not know how to change a tire, I know all about my home away from home. I don't know how to check the oil but I can tell you which flowers are which. I'm not sure where the fan belt is, but I can tell you what it sounds like when it snaps on a deserted Okanagan Valley highway on a hot weekend in July.

Anne Hughes
Vancouver, British Columbia

YEAR TEN

FIRE AND ICE

There was a December, back when I lived in Calgary, that was memorably, unbearably cold. The kind of cold that penetrates to the very core of your being and makes you think you will never get warm again. It was a real chore getting dressed to go outside each day. So many clothes. So many layers.

When I went outside on the last day of December, the sound of my boots on the crisp snow was loud and crunchy. Every footstep sounded like a firecracker. It was so cold it was hard to breathe. I had a double scarf over my mouth. Even my eyes were cold. The sky may have been blue and the sun may have been shining, but there were ice crystals floating eerily in the air like snowflakes. You could hear them hitting the ground and you could see them drifting into little piles.

Coming inside was a momentary reprieve, until you realized that even with the furnace and fireplace blazing, you had to wrap yourself in warm clothing and a comforter to feel a measure of relief.

Cold air oozed through the cracks in my front door. I taped fuzzy strips of rags around the sides of the frame and pushed a rolled rug across the bottom. It didn't make a difference. The metal door efficiently conducted the cold into the entrance and it drifted up the stairs.

And so I decided to spend New Year's Eve cocooned in my favourite chair. I would sip tea and watch TV rather than join the brave souls who congregated outside for the midnight countdown.

But I had a premonition that something wonderful might happen that New Year's Day. Sure enough, when I opened my bedroom drapes, the sky was full of grey clouds whizzing by and changing shapes. It looked like a Chinook, though the world was obviously still frozen.

Fearing I'd be greeted by an icy wind, I dressed warmly to walk to Mass. When I stepped outside, however, the sky had turned crystal clear blue. Ever so tentatively, I lowered my scarf. When I did I took a deep breath and inhaled warm, balmy air. I opened my collar and my coat, I removed my scarf and my gloves. It was like a spring day.

The squeaky crunch of frozen snow had been replaced by the sound of rustling pine—and water streaming off the trees like fountains as the ice melted.

There was not a soul on the sidewalk, nor a vehicle on the street, just the rush of warm wind and the sound of singing birds. I took a shortcut through a park and sank up to my knees through the once-hard crust. When I got to my church it took me ten minutes to cool down.

On the way home, the sun and the wind were in my face, kissing my cheeks with every step. It was an exhilarating way to start the New Year. Calgary was still sleeping, but the trees, wind, and birds were celebrating. I saw a young couple sitting on their balcony, still in their pyjamas, holding on to one another and sharing a cup of coffee. There was a faint sound of wind chimes from someone's porch. I went into my home, opened all the windows, and sat on my balcony, welcoming in the New Year, good health, and the gift of life, thankful for the unexpected blessing of a Calgary Chinook on New Year's Day.

Cathy Rakchaev
Mundare, Alberta

SITTING, STILL

Last Saturday my wife and I made a trip "up island" to say goodbye to an old friend who had finally lost her battle to cancer.

She'd lived in Ladysmith for many years, but her family's roots were up in Union Bay. We chose to leave the parkway a few miles before town and finish the journey ambling along the old island highway that hugs the water's edge. There were new homes here and there, but mostly we were driving by homes from another time: yards cluttered with pickups or tarp-covered boats waiting for spring. The kind of homes where clotheslines and wood stoves still earn their keep.

The town hall was easy to find. The parking lot was jammed and folks were standing in clusters—everyone dressed a little better than usual for a Saturday.

Inside, the warm wood walls were adorned with records of local history: plaques, pictures, and other bits and pieces. The strains of "Tell Me the Old, Old Story" came from an upright piano near the corner of the room. The scent of fresh coffee hung in the air as several women set food on side tables: egg salad, tuna, and ham sandwiches, squares, cakes, and cookies, coffee, tea, and juice for the children.

And then it was time for the service to begin. A hush fell over the room, stragglers scurried for their seats, and the minister settled into the story of my friend's life: an interesting biography to some; to others, memories both beautiful and painful.

A trio of women stood and sang. None of them had what you'd call singing voices; there was no attempt at harmonizing, they were just three cousins who wanted to present a tribute from the heart to a beloved friend.

There was a rare honesty about that gathering. That old town hall provided an atmosphere that neither church nor funeral chapel could have offered. It sits there year after year bearing silent witness to how people *really* live. It's seen a lifetime of town meetings, concerts, dances, wedding receptions and, yes, funeral services.

We live in a world hypnotized with forward motion. That old town hall has chosen to let the world rush right on by.

Rod Wotherspoon

Ladysmith, British Columbia

SKYTRAIN JUSTICE

I'm writing to tell you about an experience I had riding public transit in Vancouver.

I was on my way home from returning textbooks to the library downtown. I boarded the SkyTrain and settled in for my forty-five-minute train ride. I zoned out for a few stations and, following the social norm, avoided eye contact and conversation with the strangers around me.

An older man boarded the train. The only available seat was occupied by a knapsack. The gentleman smiled kindly at the young man whose knapsack it was and asked if he wouldn't mind moving it so he could have a seat. The young man, a twenty-something wearing a hoodie and oversized earphones, scowled up at the man and swore loudly.

The entire car went silent. The old man was so taken aback he was speechless. He turned and walked to the other side of the car. Though most of us were cursing the young man in our heads, none of us said anything aloud. After all, it was none of our business; we were just chance observers of an altercation that didn't involve us. But a third man, probably thirty-five or so, stood up.

"Excuse me?" he said, as though the affront had been directed at him.

The young man pulled his headphones down to his neck. "You talking to me?"

"Yes, I am talking to you. That is no way to treat a fellow human being. You should apologize."

The young man rudely insisted that he was not going to apologize. He had a limited vocabulary—he'd used the F-word as both verb *and* adjective.

So, Mr. Thirty-something reached right over Mr. Twenty-something's head and clicked on the SkyTrain emergency intercom.

There was static and then: "Hello, what seems to be the problem?"

He answered that there was a young man aboard the train who had just threatened an older gentleman.

The voice over the intercom promised to dispatch the SkyTrain police to meet the train at the next station. Then it asked for a description.

"He's male, about five-ten, maybe twenty-five or so, brown hair—oh and he's ugly as heck."

The young man sat bolt upright. His ears were burning pink. He looked around the train car. All eyes met his. When the train pulled into the next station, he jumped to his feet, snatched up his knapsack, and darted out of the car.

Mr. Thirty-something sat back down. The older man thanked him and took a seat. It seemed as if the entire car let out a communal sigh of relief. We were all smiling, giving each other knowing glances, and commenting on the episode to one another as if we were old friends.

A woman turned to Mr. Thirty-something, pointed to the yellow band under the window, and said, "You know, there are silent alarms."

"Oh, I know about the silent alarms. But it was public humiliation I was going for."

And that was that: one man taking SkyTrain morality into his own hands. One man willing to stand up for what was right, while the rest of us remained silent. He renewed my faith in humanity that day. And I'm sure that wherever that young man is now, the next time someone asks him to move his knapsack, he will do so.

Mindy Ogden
New Westminster, British Columbia

THE WEBS WE LEAVE

Over dinner a few weeks ago our older son, Ian, told us a story.

Ian is in his late forties, a big, burly motorcycle rider. In fact, most of Ian's stories are about his motorcycles. He owns four BMWs. All significant models, he tells us, all with complicated model names. I just refer to them as the red one, the white one, the black one, and the blue one.

Ian was heading to Vancouver on business. He would usually ride one of his motorcycles, but because of the nature of this trip he'd decided to take his car. So, he had to open the seldom-used door on the car side of his garage.

When he did, he saw a large, magnificent cobweb.

Ian's garage faces east, which means the early morning sunshine was glinting off the web. Ian was staring at a dazzling display of spider craftsmanship. The web covered not only much of the upper part of the opening, it continued beyond, toward his front door.

Ian could see the spider. He could also see that she had at least three meals lined up. Her diet for the day, he presumed. He figured that if he was very careful, and moved some motor- cycle pieces, he could manoeuvre his car out of the garage without destroying the web. When he reached the end of the steep driveway he stopped, parked, and went back to check. The web was intact. He was pleased with himself.

When he returned home that evening, there was a UPS package on his doorstep. The cobweb was gone. Ian chuckled, somewhat self-consciously, as he told us this story, but I was transported back about forty years. Because I knew why he'd taken such pains to preserve the web.

I remembered a much younger, smaller Ian, maybe seven or eight years old. It was a spring afternoon. Ian was lying on his bed, finishing what was probably the very first "real" book he'd read himself. He reached the end of the second to last chapter, lay there in complete silence for a minute, and then said, in a choked little voice, "My throat feels funny." He didn't recognize that he was on the verge of tears.

The book was *Charlotte's Web*.

Charlotte, the spider, was going to die.

Ian said the UPS driver probably didn't notice the spider's web.

But I think the driver just hadn't ever read *Charlotte's Web*.

I am reading it again.

Barbara Craigie
Bellingham, Washington

THE GIFT OF GOODBYE

I was born in a small mining town in northern Quebec. Over the years I'd often thought about going back. When the subject would come up with my dad, he'd often say, "*That* would be a great trip. Wish *I* could go." Or, "You'll have to give me a full report when you get back."

Finally, motivated partly by my guilt about things left undone and partly by my dad's declining health, my wife, Jen, and I decided to make the trip. We would ride our motorcycles. It would be a road trip in pursuit of my past.

It was perfect riding weather, and the winding roads through the rural north were smooth, scenic, and free of traffic.

After about two and a half days on the road, we rounded a familiar bend. I could see "the stacks." Two of them, exactly as I had remembered. Beacons, guiding me home to familiar addresses: Grandma and Grandpa's house, the local drugstore, a wooden sidewalk, a poisoned lake, the Anglican church where I was christened and, of course, the mine.

As well as being the only significant employer in the region, the mine had been the centre for social activities. My mom and dad met while working at the mine. My grandpa was an engineer there.

Jen and I went to the mine office to see about a tour. The receptionist politely excused herself and returned with a lady who worked in the personnel office. She was interested in my historical connection. She requested names and dates. She left us for about ten minutes, and when she returned she was holding three employment cards: 3 × 5 originals handwritten with fountain pens and complete with employment dates, home addresses, supervisor names, positions, rates of pay, raises, name changes from maiden to married, and employment end dates. I was astounded. This was a solid connection to the past and, for me, more valuable than the gold extracted in the smelters. I was anxious to share them with my dad.

When we got home I phoned to tell him about the trip and to let him know I'd mailed him a surprise package. A couple of days later my brother contacted me to say that Dad hadn't been feeling well and had been taken to the hospital for tests. I decided I should tell him about the trip and the cards in person. I hopped on my bike and headed east down the highway.

In his hospital room my dad and I shared the memories of my trip and his memories of days gone by. The employment cards stirred up stories of meeting, dating, and then marrying my mom; of winters so cold if you spat on the ground the glob would bounce; of a boyhood prank where he climbed one of the stacks; and of the two huskies that used to pull him and his sled across the lake to school and back.

Although we had a good relationship, I never felt as close to my dad as I did when he painted those pictures of his life in the north. It was a connection for both of us. Father to son; man to man; friend to friend. The memories and stories continued pouring out over the next two days.

And then Dad's test results came. His kidneys were failing fast. His bladder was infected. His lungs were operating at only ten percent. It was clear he wasn't getting out of the hospital. The rest of the family was called as the doctor reviewed his findings with my dad. Realizing his situation, Dad made a decision not to resuscitate. And he resigned himself to the wait. The next day, with his family at his side and an Anglican priest guiding his soul, Dad let go and passed away. The employment cards were sitting on the bedside table.

Norm Perkins

Don Mills, Ontario

MISDIRECTION

I work on the east side of Vancouver's Gastown. It isn't quite the Downtown Eastside, but it's close. My office is near the new Woodward's Building, the statue of Gassy Jack, and an ever-increasing number of coffee shops, restaurants, and furniture stores that have opened in the last while.

A couple of floors in the building are being renovated for a high-tech movie company; fibre-optic cable is being pulled and the old warehouse space is being updated. During the work, a security guard has been hired to watch the front door of the building. He's about five-six and may weigh 140 pounds on a good day. He wears a black-and-white uniform that hangs on him and military-style black leather shoes that are always polished and proper.

It's a little unclear to me what form of security he provides. The door to the building is locked and people either get in with a security swipe card or they're buzzed in by a tenant in the building. I guess he was hired to watch out for people who may sneak in after others swipe or get buzzed.

Our security guard soon became a welcome addition. He brightened up those moments as you rush to get out of the rain and into the warm. He offered a smile, commented on the weather, and wished you a good day.

After a few weeks, he took it upon himself to open the door for people. I think he liked this progression from security guard to doorman. He took to it as though this was really what he was there to do. He started by opening the door for people who were getting their swipe card out of their pocket. And then he started opening the door for people he recognized. And then he started opening the door for the construction workers, or the people who looked like they may be construction workers.

Before long there were complaints that people were being let into the building willy-nilly, people who were just trying to get warm.

Someone spoke to our security guard. I don't know who it was, but it became obvious when I came to work this morning that something had changed. Instead of standing by the door, he was back on his stool. And he didn't get up to open the door for me. He still gave me a smile, but it was clear that things weren't the same.

He seemed slightly hardened. He carried himself in a way that said he now knew what was and wasn't expected of him. And that he'd lost something he was looking for.

Stephen Smith

North Vancouver, British Columbia

A CHRISTMAS PRAYER

In 1955 I was a Mountie in charge of an RCMP detachment in the Interlake area of Manitoba. We received very heavy snow in November and December of that year, and travel in some rural areas was difficult. Nevertheless, on December 24, true to a commitment we'd made, we went around the area delivering clothing we'd gathered, wooden toys we'd made, festive food, and turkeys.

Most of the houses were easily reached by car, but there was one that wasn't. It was on a little-used bush road about four miles from town. It was home to a single mother and four children, ranging in age from one to eight. They had no telephone.

I had one of the junior constables with me. We drove to the closest store to inquire about the exact location of the home.

The storekeeper drew a map for us and said we'd be able to drive about three miles north, but that the family lived on a side road that hadn't been plowed, so we'd have to walk from there. He was concerned because he hadn't heard anything from them for two weeks. He gave us some candy and nuts to add to our gifts.

It was nearly seven o'clock. It was dark and it was cold. But there was a bit of a moon.

We managed the three miles without difficulty, but at the side road our hearts sank. The road was filled with snow; there wasn't even a trail.

We started out. The snow was over our knees in most places, and it was hard going. We could scarcely see, and we were afraid we would miss the house. We considered turning back.

I guess the thoughts of my own children kept me going. Finally we saw a light through the trees, and a short time later, a small cabin.

Exhausted, we struggled through a gate in the wire fence and stumbled our way up to the house. Inside we could hear children's voices. We knocked. There was complete silence for a few moments, and then the door slowly opened.

It must have been a shock for that little family to see two burly policemen dressed in buffalo coats. They looked apprehensive, but when they saw our sleigh and the box of presents, their expressions changed to amazement and joy. One little voice cried, "See, Mama, Santa Claus did come!"

The mother burst into tears. She threw her arms around us and kissed us soundly.

"You are an answer to our prayers," she said.

Through her tears she told us she'd tried to explain to the children that Santa wouldn't be able to find them this year with all the snow, and there wouldn't be any presents or Christmas dinner. The children didn't believe her. The oldest boy said, "We can always pray." And he insisted they all kneel down.

The mother agreed, but she dreaded the disappointment they would suffer when their prayers weren't answered.

"We had hardly said 'Amen' when you knocked on the door," she told us.

With joy in our hearts we laid out the big turkey and other food and gifts. We were smothered with hugs and kisses from the four little kids. Everyone shed tears of joy.

The trip from the car to the house had been a struggle every step of the way. But we were so overwhelmed by the Christmas spirit that we floated back to our vehicle.

The next day, Christmas with my wife and three little boys was made even more joyful by the memory of the four little faces in that humble cottage way out there in the bush. By that, and by their faith in the spirit of Christmas.

William LaMar Palmer

Brandon, Manitoba
(submitted by his son Bruce Palmer of Brandon, Manitoba)

AND THE BAND PLAYED ON

When I was a boy, I felt a strong sense of empathy for the old folks at Sunset Lodge. Twice a day, on my way to and from Queen Charlotte Junior High in Charlottetown, I rattled past the motel-like seniors' residence in a big school bus.

There never seemed to be much action at Sunset Lodge. The west-facing picture windows were draped, even at dusk. The facade was tired and worn.

In grade seven I was a proud new trumpeter in the school band. My musical career was inspired by my preacher grandfather, who'd learned to sing and play from *his* father in the coal towns of central Wales. I was happy to carry on the tradition and excited to be in the concert band that Christmas. In those years I was a quiet and sensitive young man, but I had good chops. And one day, around the middle of December, I figured I had an idea for how to bring empathy and my new-found talent together.

I assembled some band members and proposed a pre-Christmas mission: we'd put together a grade seven ensemble to play for the residents at Sunset Lodge. It seemed like the right thing to do—to bring our youthful Christmas joy to the old folks! Within a day, our little troupe had gelled. Melanie would play clarinet; Helen, the French horn. Lance volunteered to be our trombone, Zoe would add the perky piccolo. I, of course, had my shiny new trumpet.

It was perfect.

Late in the week I snuck out of class early to drop by Sunset Lodge and pitch my plan. The management embraced the idea.

A few days later, when we arrived for our evening performance, a ragtag gaggle of residents had assembled in anticipation. The crowd was fanned out around a little stage— on stretchers, in wheelchairs, and propped against the walls, gripping IV racks. It was very quiet. We were scared stiff.

We set up our folding stands and sheet music, and selected our first piece.

"Deck the Halls" seemed like a good choice to get things going—a rousing carol, celebratory, and familiar to all. I tapped my toe to set the 4/4 time. We began. In absolute silence. Silence, which was followed by two foghorn honks from Helen, which was followed by more silence, and then more, and then a whimsical piccolo peep from Zoe, and then three of us in unison playing the last four "las" of "Fa-la-la-la-laa, la-la-la-la."

In horror, we realized that the grade seven kids are rarely assigned the melody in junior high concert band. That was the sacred space for the seasoned older grades. The melody notes for all the tunes we planned to play were missing. Our parts were all harmony: the flourishes. In my haste I had assembled a band made up of my friends, all of them backup players. Collectively, we represented the animal sounds of "Away in a Manger," the cracking whip of "Jingle Bells," and those last four "las" in "Deck the Halls."

Nevertheless, we soldiered on, red-faced at our own short-sightedness.

Amazingly, the seniors didn't seem to mind. They clapped and rocked and smiled. They encouraged us. To fill in the gaps, we began to sing and hum the melodies. Soon, everybody was singing. Over the next forty-five minutes of honking, and tooting, and singing, we played our repertoire of Christmas favourites. More than once. More staff and residents shuffled by and joined in. Our spirits soared. It was a Christmas miracle! It ended with hearty applause, hugs, date squares, and sugar cookies. Our mission was complete.

Stuart Hickox

Ottawa, Ontario

PUDDING IN
THE POST

In 1984 my sister Elizabeth followed family tradition and took to the road.

Having covered most of Europe on a previous adventure, she and a friend headed for India—the first stop on a year-long adventure that was to end, finally, in England.

We had all *begun* in England, and were, in some ways, still English to the core. And never more so than at Christmas. Christmas in our house was mincemeat pies, fruitcakes of all different weights and colours, and of course plum pudding, hot and slathered in brandy butter. My mother always began her preparations in early fall, never deviating from the recipes, tried and true.

That year, as a special surprise for Elizabeth, Mom decided to make an extra pudding and mail it to India. To Bombay to be precise, where Elizabeth thought she'd be for the holidays. Before the days of email and Facebook, leaving forwarding addresses was the only way that longed-for news of home could find you. Phone calls were only for emergencies.

The pudding mix was prepared as always, though to ward

off tropical bugs my mother mixed in a triple dose of brandy. She also used extra wrapping: she doubled the cheesecloth, the cotton, and the tinfoil. She placed the cake in a sturdy box, wrapped it in brown paper, tied it with string, and carefully printed the addresses: a return one for Victoria and an exotic outward-bound one for India. Into the mail it went with crossed fingers and a stunning amount of postage.

Elizabeth didn't get it.

Rude words were muttered that Christmas about the efficiency of post offices everywhere. Evil thoughts slipped in of someone in a dead-letter office enjoying a wayward Christmas treat.

The New Year came, Elizabeth returned from her travels, and the pud was forgotten.

And then, almost a year later, I looked out the front window to see my mother, a package in her hand, laughing her way up the driveway. The outside wrapper was clean, marked with only two addresses: my mother's here in Victoria and her sister's in England. Inside was a wonder. The box with the Christmas pudding had followed my sister for a year, every forwarding address clearly written, every missed address carefully crossed out: New Delhi, Kathmandu, Christchurch, Sydney, Darwin, the Cook Islands, Tahiti, Fiji, Honolulu, and more, until it had reached England with not an inch of space left. My aunt, intrigued, had rewrapped it and sent it once more on its way, new postage attached.

The pudding, though completely desiccated, was still in one piece. My mother, firmly of the waste not, want not generation, tucked the pudding into the cupboard: Christmas was coming around again. Sure enough, on Christmas Day, she steamed it for an extra long time, both to rehydrate it and to dispatch anything untoward that might have survived the desiccation. Then she served it, with great flair and fully aflame, to a very skeptical table.

It was delicious.

Jane Jile

Victoria, British Columbia

THE LIVES OF OTHERS

It was the summer of 1967, a summer of excitement and pride across Canada, and there were few more exciting places to work than at Expo 67 in Montreal.

I had the privilege of being part of the Canadian Pavilion for the duration of the World Fair. I was to be a mounted rider with the Royal Canadian Mounted Police.

Opening day began with exploding mortars and low-level fly-pasts by the Golden Centennaires aerobatic team. Since the plan called for us to be isolated from the public, our horse stand was in a large, elevated sandbox. The horses, however, quickly let it be known that the perch was not to their liking, so authorities hurriedly decided to bring us down into the plaza. This created a new problem. Because there was no separation from the public, we had to ensure that no toes were stepped on and that our horses didn't spook. To do that, we had to decide when it was safe to let people close to us, and when it wasn't.

One afternoon I noticed a boy, maybe ten or twelve years old, sitting quietly in a wheelchair outside the throng that was surrounding my horse. I carefully moved toward the boy, watching for clues from his parents in case I was getting *too* close.

I asked if their son would like to touch the animal. They nodded. My horse lowered his head and began gently nibbling the boy's fingers. The broad smile on his face turned to uncontrolled, hearty laughter. I allowed it to continue for longer than normal before I turned to greet others. As I did I felt a pang of concern, because I saw both parents weeping as they moved away.

A couple of hours later I rode behind the pavilion to give my horse a chance to get a drink and stretch its back. I had dismounted and was beginning my chores when I saw the boy and his family coming toward me. Both parents were still noticeably emotional.

To my astonishment they told me that that moment in the plaza was the first time they had ever seen their son laugh.

They told me they were incredibly thankful to have discovered what could bring him joy.

Treats for horses were reserved for special occasions, and I figured no occasion could be more special than this. I dug out some horse treats and we all shared the boy's delight as my horse gingerly picked them off the palm of his outstretched hand. I confess that I required a couple of minutes to regain my own composure before going back out front.

I had learned an important lesson that day. I learned what impact seemingly insignificant gestures can have on the lives of others.

Don Buchanan

Coldstream, British Columbia

LIST OF CONTRIBUTORS